"Newman has given us a well-written book full of wisdom on how to accomplish a very difficult task—witness to our own relatives. The pages are lucid, wise, honest, humorous, and convicting all at once. The stories of successes and failures powerfully hit home. The suggestions of leading questions and ideas for sharing the faith at the end of the chapters are outstanding. I believe God will use this wonderful book to lead many relatives to Christ."

Robert Peterson, independent researcher,
St. Louis, Missouri

"*Bringing the Gospel Home* keeps its promise to give hope to Christians who long to see family members come to Christ. Newman builds his approach on solid theology, offers sound advice, and highlights his insights with rich stories that connect head and heart in the art of bringing people to Jesus. The methods in this book, while focused on winning family, are easily transferable to sharing the gospel with anyone. I recommend this book to all who want to increase their skills at sharing the good news with others."

Jerry Root, Associate Professor of Evangelism and Leadership,
Wheaton College; coauthor, *The Sacrament of Evangelism*

"Pastoring in a city that can be political to the point of being polemical, and diplomatic to the point of being deceitful, I tend to notice those people who embody truth-loving tact. Randy Newman is one of those people. And his skill at sharing the gospel is exemplary. Here, Newman shows us how to witness boldly and winsomely to our nonbelieving family members. Many would benefit by reading this book."

John Yates, Rector, The Falls Church, Falls Church, Virginia

"Newman has challenged and charmed lay audiences as a plenary speaker at apologetics conferences sponsored by the Evangelical Philosophical Society. His approach to evangelism is a wonderful blend of thoughtful faith and deep compassion for people. You will be inspired by his insights."

William Lane Craig, Research Professor of Philosophy,
Talbot School of Theology;
founder, Reasonable Faith, www.reasonablefaith.org

"This is one scary title. But if you think you've got a story to tell about family versus faith, listen to Randy's own, and the others he's collected here. And hear his hopeful and wise reflections. They will help you out of the sticky place you're in."

C. John Sommerville, Professor Emeritus of English History, University of Florida; author, *How the News Makes Us Dumb*

"*Listening* is as much of persuasion—perhaps more—as is *explaining*. Newman shows how we can engage our families winsomely, respectfully, and with the grace and truth that alone can transform lives for eternity. Introducing loved ones to Jesus can be as difficult as it is imperative. *Bringing the Gospel Home* provides us with a user-friendly roadmap."

Robert Schwarzwalder, Senior Vice President, Family Research Council

BRINGING THE
GOSPEL
H🏠ME

ACKNOWLEDGMENTS

Behind every book stands a cast of characters who made it possible. This one is no exception. First, I am thankful for the many people who shared their stories with me about witnessing to their family. Many of them cried. Their vulnerability and compassion for their relatives moved me greatly.

My second family, the Olive Tree Congregation, lovingly led by my dear friends Dan and Cynthia Strull, provided me with a home away from home and lots of prayer while working on this book.

Many friends encouraged me greatly while writing. I offer thanks for the strength I gained from Spencer Brand, Patrick Dennis, Mark Petersburg, Lin Johnson, Glenn Oeland, the Washington, DC, Campus Crusade staff team, my Faculty Commons co-laborers, our church couples' group, and the George Mason Faculty Fellowship.

I am grateful to God for shaping my thinking through three important influences: the sermons of Tim Keller, the theological writings of D. A. Carson, and just about every word written by or about C. S. Lewis.

And how could I write a book about family without acknowledging how thankful I am for mine?

Mom and Dad, thank you for thinking so highly of me and letting me know you think I'm great. You're deluded, of course. But I'm thankful to God for your love for me.

Barry, Ellen, Brian, and Susy, thank you for valuing family so much that you're willing to travel ridiculous amounts of miles just to have Chinese food together.

Dan, David, and Jon, thank you for providing nonstop joy and "outright prolonged laughter."

And, Pam, thank you for being a woman of valor, the wife of my youth, my most serious critic, my most diligent proofreader, my biggest cheerleader, and my dearest life partner. Without you, I wouldn't value family enough to write this book, feel confident enough to express myself, or enjoy family enough to want others do the same.

INTRODUCTION

When I informed a friend I was writing a book on witnessing to family, he told me he had the perfect chapter titles:

Chapter 1: Don't Do It!
Chapter 2: Don't Do It!
Chapter 3: Did You Think I Was Kidding?
Chapter 4: Pray for Somebody Else to Do It
Chapter 5: Review Chapters 1, 2, and 3

He then offered several firsthand stories of how *not* to witness to family. And he had more from where those came from. Since then, many others have volunteered the same kinds of illustrations. Apparently, horror stories outnumber success stories.

This hasn't deterred me. In fact, it has propelled me to write this book with a sense of urgency. Since my first book, *Questioning Evangelism*, was published in 2004, God has opened up many opportunities for me to speak about witnessing. During the question-and-answer periods that follow my presentations, inquiries about reaching out to family with the gospel have always been the most frequent and painful questions posed. People want to know how they can engage their loved ones with the good news. After my presentations, people come up to tell me, through tears, of their atheistic father or bitter mother or gay brother or drug-addicted sister

". . . but please talk about something else . . . *anything* else." I got the message. Jesus was off limits.

That didn't stop me from sending books, pamphlets, and long letters imploring my parents to be true to their Jewish roots and embrace the Jewish Messiah who was promised by Jewish prophets.

Once I even sent them the Jesus film, a presentation of the Gospel of Luke, in Hebrew. (I had already sent them a copy of the film in English, which they didn't watch). My parents don't speak a word of Hebrew, but somehow I thought they'd be impressed that Jesus spoke the same language as Moses. Of course, the fact that the Hebrew was dubbed into the film didn't seem to deter me from sending it. They never watched the Hebrew version either. Like its English counterpart, it collected dust on the shelf near their television.

Once I invited my parents to a Messianic Jewish congregation's Friday night worship service. They walked out.

I also sent them a copy of my favorite book for telling Jewish people about the gospel, Stan Telchin's *Betrayed*. It's a masterfully crafted intertwining of the author's testimony with biblical arguments for the messiahship of Jesus. Telchin tells of his daughter's going away to college and finding Jesus, an offense to his Jewish sensibilities that needed to be countered. He felt "betrayed" and set out on a year-long research project to prove his daughter wrong. What he found, instead, was irrefutable and irresistible evidence that led him, his wife, and their other daughter to faith in the Messiah. His book has been used countless times to lead Jewish people to faith. Surely, I thought, a book as wonderful as this would be the silver bullet that would usher my parents into the fold. My mother read it, made no comment, and then gave it away to someone who she said, "really needed something like that."

Nothing worked. For decades. All the "frontal assaults" failed to have any kind of impact. To be honest, I have to tell you that at some point I gave up hope. I stopped praying and probably harbored some bitterness toward God that he hadn't chosen my parents to be among the elect.

Then one day my Mom and I had a pivotal phone conversation. She recounted an experience she had at a funeral for a teacher at the high school I had attended. I knew this man. He was a sarcastic, bitter atheist who suffered for over two years as a debilitating cancer ate away at his body. Hearing the reports of his gradual demise was a painful process. Worse than the medical aspects of the story were the spiritual ones. He never softened as he approached death. In fact, it would be more accurate to say that he grew in bitterness as the end approached.

My mother, whose religious philosophy at the time could be summed up as "everyone goes to heaven," told me of her attempts to comfort the deceased man's grieving adult children.

"Don't worry," she told them, "at least now your father is in a better place."

Their response surprised my mother. Having embraced their father's skepticism, they rolled their eyes in disdain for my mother's naiveté and rudely walked away from her. She told this, I believe, to elicit some sympathy from me. After all, I was her "religious" son, and I certainly would give credence to her attempts to point atheists toward the supernatural.

I was torn. I was grateful that my mother thought about the afterlife. But I couldn't help thinking about numerous passages of Scripture that argue the exact opposite of my mom's position. Indeed I did not believe my former teacher was in a better place. I had visions of flames and worms and gnashing of teeth. I wanted to preach an entire sermon, right there and then, on the phone, about everlasting torment, wrath, and sulfur.

I opted, instead, to ask my mother a question.

"Mom, how do you know that?"

Long pause.

"How do I know what?" she replied.

"How do you know he's in a better place? It sounds like you know that with a great deal of confidence. What makes you so sure?"

I should tell you that Jewish-Mother-guilt can be conveyed with silence, even over the telephone, just as powerfully as face to face. I knew my mother was upset with me. But I also knew that, for seventy years, she had been stuck in a religious frame of reference that needed to be challenged. If not now, when?

Finally, she said, "I guess I don't know that."

This was a breakthrough. Nothing I had ever said, sent, diagramed, or preached had ever seemed to get through. This was different. She budged from confident assurance of belief in a lie to an uncomfortable doubt that could lead to searching and questioning. I wanted to sing the Hallelujah chorus!

The rest of our phone call was strained. Somewhere in there I elaborated, "Well, maybe you should do some research about this." In just a few minutes, we hung up. But I was thankful that something had finally shaken my mother's naïve confidence. Maybe, just maybe, she was beginning to doubt that anyone could go to heaven, regardless of his life's experiences or faith position.

We didn't talk about matters of faith for a very long time after that phone call. And then my parents bought their first computer. They signed up for Internet service and learned how to send me e-mail . . . lots of e-mail . . . most of which had musical attachments. Suddenly, a mode of communication opened up between my mother and me that didn't seem threatening to her. She was able to express doubts and ask questions with less fear than ever. Mind you, she was now seventy-one years old and this was more than twenty years after I had become a believer.

One day my mother sent me an e-mail that read, "I think I might try to read the New Testament." I wanted to print that e-mail and frame it. "Well, I'd love to hear what you think about it, Mom," I replied, trying to understate my enthusiasm. Over the next year, our e-mails contained frequent interaction about Jesus in the Gospels. Her questions were challenging:

"Why did Jesus say you should hate your father and mother?"

"Why did people try to kill him so many times?"

"What's so good about turning the other cheek?"

I resisted the temptation to just give answers. I found that answering her questions with questions was more productive. Not only was this a very Jewish style of communication, but it engaged her in the thinking process far better than just telling her what I thought. So I hit reply and typed out things like:

"Why do you think Jesus said such an outrageous thing?"

"What was it about Jesus' claims that would bother people so much?"

"What could be some possible advantages to turning the other cheek? What alternative would be better?"

For months our "dialogues" forced her to think differently than she had for seven decades. Along the way, I started praying for her salvation—again. In fact, my prayers became more focused and earnest. Could it actually be that my Jewish mother could come to faith? Is God that powerful? Is he that good?

The next framable e-mail my mother sent read, "I think I'm beginning to think like you, Randy, that Jesus was the Messiah." I quickly replied, "Would you say that he's *your* Messiah?" She responded, "Not yet."

But one day, just as unexpectedly as every other step along the way, my mother asked me if I'd ever heard of a book called *Betrayed* by some guy named Stan Telchin. (There are advantages to communicating by e-mail. It allows you to yell things out loud like, "Well, yes, of course I've heard of that book. I gave you a copy of it years ago and you gave it away to someone else!" Then, after you get that kind of outburst out of the way, you can calmly hit reply and type, "Yes. I think I have heard about it. Why do you ask?")

A few more e-mails explained why she liked the book so much and how she appreciated getting it from a friend who had written a personalized note inside the cover, and that the book had sat on her shelf for at least five years, and that she'd like to discuss it over the phone with me sometime. I couldn't wait.

That phone call had all the markings of supernatural intervention about it. My mother's eyes had been opened. God's timing is not my timing, his ways are not my ways, and, best of all, his power is not my power. There was a gentleness in my mother's voice that gave evidence of new life. I almost fell to my knees when I heard her say, "My only problem is knowing that I'm going to get opposition from all my Jewish friends and relatives when I tell them that now I'm a believer in Jesus. But I guess God will help me with that too." Chokingly, I said, "Yes. I'm sure he will."

A short time later, my mother was baptized—by my brother who had become a Christian and was serving as a pastor in the Netherlands. (Yes. The brother my parents told me to stay away from! That's another story. I'll share that later.) Whenever I'm in the mood to cry, I pop open the photo, stored on my computer, of my mother being baptized by my brother.

Some Assumptions of This Book

Watching my seventy-five-year-old Jewish mother come to faith, and somehow, mysteriously, having God involve me in the process, has taught me numerous lessons. I've seen the value of patience, the significance of prayer, the marvel of grace, and the power of love. I'll share some more insights about those lessons, along with many others, throughout this book. But allow me to share some insight on how I think about this whole process before going any further. Three foundational assumptions shape my view of telling your earthly family about your heavenly father.

First, I realize that most Christians are not evangelists. Consequently, for them evangelism is not easy. A problem often arises because many of the people who speak and write about evangelism *are* evangelists. For them, evangelism *is* easy. It's as natural as breathing. They can't imagine not witnessing to anyone and everyone who comes their way. They tend to make the rest of us feel guilty.

They say, "I cannot sleep at night unless I have witnessed to at least one soul that day." When I hear that (and I have found I am not alone), I usually think, "I sleep just fine!" Or they tell how they *always* pray for a witnessing opportunity as soon as they sit down at their seat on an airplane. I pray for there to be an empty seat next to me.

When we're told that witnessing should come naturally, we're set up for failure and frustration. For the vast majority of Christians, evangelism never seems natural and never flows easily. As a result we fall into one of several pits. Either we sound like someone we're not, evangelizing with a different tone of voice than we use for every other topic. Or we wait for it to "feel right" or easy and, when that doesn't happen, we clam up. Or we beat up on ourselves for not being bold enough, smart enough, or quick enough. Thus we tell people "good news" but sound more racked with guilt than liberated by grace.

These are just the potential problems with witnessing to strangers or acquaintances. Witnessing to family members—the ones who have known us the longest, seen us at our worst, and are the least likely to fall for our facades—seems infinitely more daunting. To help you tackle this all-important task,

I have included three ingredients in each chapter: insights from the Scriptures, stories of others who have learned some lessons along the way, and specific steps you can take to make progress in bringing the gospel home.

Second, you might have expected this book to be organized differently. Perhaps you thought there'd be one chapter on witnessing to parents, one on siblings, one on aging grandparents, etc. I considered this but saw at least two problems with that approach. The bigger problem is that the issues really don't break up that way. There are so many over-arching dynamics that transcend specific relationships. The more I talked to people who had seen loved ones come to faith, the more I observed themes that applied to both parents and children, brothers and sisters, the aging and the immature, etc. It seemed more helpful to examine universal factors like grace, truth, love, humility, time, eternity, and hope. Wrestling with these issues may prove more helpful than mere "how-to" recipes of "say this," "don't say this," "remember to do this."

If the chapters were about specific relationships, a smaller, yet significant problem could arise. You might merely read *just* the chapter that you thought applied to you and miss out on the insight shared in the other sections. Even worse, you could simply pick this book up in a bookstore, skim only "your" chapter and, horror of all horrors, not buy the book! We simply can't have that.

Third, it is important to remember that this book is far more about God and the gospel than it is about you and your family. I wrestle with weightier matters than mere relational dynamics in these pages. All of the chapters contain some theological reflection to put a frame around the practical instruction about evangelism. Please be patient. You might be tempted to skip the theological parts. But a richer understanding of biblical truth, I have found, can provide a firmer foundation for bold witness and clear communication.

Besides, many people reject the gospel today because they think Christians are shallow simpletons. In many cases, they have a legitimate gripe. Let's stop giving them ammunition for that charge and instead dig deeper into the Scriptures and think biblically about all of life.

The first few chapters especially focus more on your understanding of the gospel than your sharing of the good news. It would be the height of irony to speak of sharing the message of God's gracious offer of salvation but point the spotlight on you. My hope is to avoid a common trap when teaching about evangelism—that is, to leave you obsessed with how *you're* coming across, what *you* should say, what *you* must remember, what *you* need to feel, say, and do, and when *you* need to be bolder, smarter, quicker, and holier.

Instead, my hope is that grace will amaze you more than ever. My prayer is that God's love will spill over into your conversations, gratitude will infuse your prayers, joy will transform your tone of voice and, like the prophet Micah, you will praise God and say: "Who is a God like you, who pardons sin and forgives the transgression of the remnant of his inheritance? You do not stay angry forever but delight to show mercy" (Mic. 7:18, NIV).

FAMILY

A Beatitude and Yet a Burden

Paulette came home for Christmas break from her freshman year of college armed with enough evangelistic tracts for each of her siblings.[1] Her two sisters and one brother were going to hear the gospel whether they wanted to or not. After all, this method of sharing the gospel in concise booklet form had worked in her life.

Having been raised in a nominal Christian family that occasionally attended church (and a rather liberal one at that), she had gone off to college with no interest in God or religion. But a campus evangelist caught her attention and started getting through to her. As she listened to his logical, intellectually respectable evidence for the resurrection of Jesus, she thought he was proclaiming a "new religion." At least, it was new to her.

This was no open-air ranting lunatic. He spoke calmly and reasonably to a packed audience in the university's student center auditorium and handed out comment cards for people

---

[1] Unless otherwise noted, I've changed the names of people I've used in illustrations, and, in most cases, I've changed enough details of their stories to protect their anonymity.

to indicate interest in further discussion. Paulette couldn't believe her eyes as she watched her hand writing her name and dorm address on the card and check the box marked "more information." Less than one week later, two girls stopped by her room and presented the good news by doing something anyone could do: they read a short booklet and asked Paulette if she'd like to pray the prayer on the last page.

She did and she prayed and it changed her life.

So certainly the same pattern would play itself out back at home. She lined up her three younger siblings against the wall of her bedroom (after making sure that Mom and Dad were nowhere in sight). She gave them each their own copy of the booklet and read each page aloud. The fifteen- and thirteen-year-old sisters and the ten-year-old brother cowered in submission under their big sister's orders to listen. When she asked them if they'd like to pray the prayer, they all said yes. Paulette was elated (and relieved). Not only were her precious sisters and darling brother joining her in this newfound faith, but this method of evangelism had not let her down.

That was over thirty years ago and her faith has remained strong.

But the fruit from her evangelistic lineup did not endure. The elder of the two sisters continued to drink her way through high school, went off to college and partied with the best of them, and only calmed down years later—after finding peace and tranquility in the New Age movement. The younger sister puzzled everyone in the family for years because, despite her good looks, she never had a boyfriend. When she told everyone she was a lesbian, that all made sense. And Paulette's little baby brother, who showed signs of intense devotion to Christ throughout his entire four years of college, one day decided the Christian faith just doesn't work, walked away from his marriage to a Christian woman, and still finds more relevance in secular motivational speakers than in the Scriptures.

Paulette now regrets her lining up of relatives against the wall and would urge Christians to find other strategies. This book is an attempt to explore those other methods. But before we launch into that part of the task, a bit of study about the nature of the family and the truth of the gospel needs to set the stage for training and how-tos.[2]

God's Plan for the Family

A singles' pastor once told me, "There's no drama like family drama." Ever since, I've wondered why this is so. Perhaps it is because the stakes are so high. God's design for the family is so important, so profound, and so powerful that the Devil points his most potent weapons at this most crucial target. Given that scenario, it is no wonder we feel like we're on a contested, spiritual battlefield more often than at a serene, Norman Rockwellesque dinner table.

A full appreciation for why God loves families so much and why the Evil One hates them so much sets an important backdrop for our investigation of how to share the good news with our relatives.

Family Is Important

Our discussion of the high value God places upon the family must begin with a look at the very nature of a Trinitarian God. He calls himself "Father, Son, and Holy Spirit."[3] He could have chosen terms other than ones related to family. But he

---

[2] Please don't conclude that the use of booklets is always a bad method of evangelism. It can be the perfect tool in the right setting. See Owen's story later in this chapter. No single method fits all situations. Jesus' examples of addressing different people in different ways to proclaim the same message validates a variety of methods for this all-important task.

[3] Those who suggest avoiding emotionally charged terms like "father," "son," and "Holy Spirit" by replacing them with "Creator, Redeemer, and Sustainer" make too great a sacrifice at the altar of cultural relevance. To be sure, God is indeed Creator, Redeemer, and Sustainer. He himself validates those titles—but not as replacements for Father, Son, and Holy Spirit. Jesus' authoritative use of "Father" points us to its primacy as a title, which must not be censored, avoided, or even minimized. We dare not let this world's devaluing of the family dictate our views, values, or choice of vocabulary.

didn't. Even though the title of "father" is found less often in the Old Testament than in the New, it is not out of place in the books of the law, the prophets, and the writings. The notion that God can be understood as a caring, nurturing, protecting Abba pervades both testaments.

Just one example, a rather substantial one, should suffice for our argument. When the prophet Isaiah arrived at that climactic moment of his Immanuel prophecy, declaring that the Messiah will be with us, he revealed God's trust-inspiring titles of "Wonder-Counselor, Almighty-God, *Eternal-Father*, Prince-of-Peace" (Isa. 9:6, my translation). Right there in the midst of some of the loftiest titles of deity stands the label "Father."

Thus, it is not without scriptural warrant that the Jewish community crafted and recites one of its holiest prayers, Avinu, Malkenu—"Our Father, Our King." The rabbis of old recognized God's immanent, gentle, and intimate nature found in his title "father" as well as his transcendent, royal, and holy nature seen in "king." He is both loving and ruling, to be trusted and revered, the one we rest in and bow before. Our response to him is both as sons and servants, children and worshipers, in delight and in awe.

Jesus' frequent use of the term "Father" for the first person of the Trinity was consistent with the Old Testament's depiction of God as one who "is gracious and compassionate . . . faithful to all his promises and loving toward all he has made . . . upholds all those who fall . . . and watches over all who love him . . ." (Ps. 145:8, 13–14, 20, NIV).[4]

No wonder Paul connects the divine pattern to every earthly family in his prayer for the Ephesians, where he petitions "the Father, from whom every family in heaven and on earth is named" (Eph. 3:15) for strength, stability, grounding, and comprehension of God's love (see Eph. 3:14–19).

---

[4] It would not be difficult to find dozens, if not hundreds, of other verses that praise God for his father-like care and compassion.

When families fulfill their God-ordained purposes, this kind of strength flows to and through all members in beautiful ways.

Consider some of the other family terminology linked to profound truths in the Scriptures. Those redeemed by the blood of Christ are called "sons" who have been "adopted." The church is referred to as the "bride of Christ." And, when all of time is culminated, at what kind of banquet will we feast? A "marriage supper."

The point not to be missed is that the image of family is woven into the revelation of the godhead and displayed at crucial junctures of God's written Word. Therefore, we must treat family with reverence and awe. It is a divinely ordained and shaped institution, not merely some culturally constructed convention that needs to be tolerated.

There are at least two implications of God's Trinitarian nature upon our reflections about family. First, since God is relational, we who are created in his image are also relational. We are hard-wired for communal connections, of which family ties are the most intimate and important. Second, since God is others-oriented (the Father reveals the Son, the Son submits to the Father, the Holy Spirit seeks to bring glory to the Son, etc.), so we should be others-oriented. Selflessness validates our image-of-God-bearing nature. Selfishness violates it. Living our lives theocentrically, the ultimate display of other-centeredness, resonates with our very nature, our reason for being, and our deepest longings.

All this is to say that family dynamics weigh heavily in our lives. We who have been chosen by a heavenly Father, redeemed by an atoning Son, and sealed with a Holy Spirit should value family highly. Despite all the cultural trends that serve to lampoon and demean the institution of the family (even if we imagine our specific family's portrait in the dictionary next to the word "dysfunctional"), we who have experienced the unmerited favor of God must look to him for the resources to uphold the high regard for this divinely ordained, all-important institution.

Family Is Intimate

When God established the family, he started with the most basic unit—a marriage between a man and a woman. He rolled out the blueprint for all time with this prescription: "a man shall leave his father and his mother and hold fast to his wife, and they shall become one flesh" (Gen. 2:24). When Jesus was challenged about possible escape clauses allowing for a divorce, he appealed to this "one-flesh" intimacy as the basis for preserving a marriage. When Paul argued against uniting with a prostitute, he recalled this "one-flesh" imagery as proof that mere "casual sex" was an impossibility and an oxymoron.

God further described intimacy as shamelessness by adding, "And the man and his wife were both naked and were not ashamed" (Gen. 2:25). These poetic statements imply far more than just sexual union. The man and the woman enjoyed unhindered oneness in all dimensions of their beings. They felt no need to hide from each other using fig leaves, lies, emotional withdrawal, or pretense. Adam and Eve had no need to explain, clarify, restate, employ active listening skills, offer alibis, or ever say, "You should be ashamed of yourself."

Just recently, I watched a pastor and his wife receive a standing ovation from their congregation as appreciation for over thirty years of caring for the church. The applause also rose out of gratitude for their modeling a marriage that endured through trials and pains. As the volume in the sanctuary rose to a level preventing anyone from overhearing, the husband whispered something in the ear of his bride. She laughed and the two of them exchanged a look that could only come after decades of intimacy. No one else knew what he said or what she thought, but we all felt a sense of awe for the intimacy these two had forged along the way.

Among the many disastrous results of Adam and Eve's rebellion against God, painfully recounted in Genesis 3, are the impulses to hide from one another (hence the fig leaves). In other words, the fall brought about a marring of the one-flesh intimacy God intended as the foundation for family.

While obviously not to the level of sexual intimacy, a kind of openness and unashamedness should pass down from the intimate couple to all of the family, thus creating a kind of greenhouse that fosters trust, depth of communication, and a joy found nowhere else.

Please don't miss my point. Families were instituted by God to foster intimacy, to build trust, to be the springboard from which all relationships should work, and to bring about connectedness between people. The Devil hates such goals and continues to do all he can to make families into sources of alienation rather than intimacy.

Family Makes an Impression

Families also serve as God's training centers. Consider the many verses in Proverbs that portray the family as the setting for promoting wisdom, developing discernment, acquiring prudence, and establishing the fear of the Lord. Relational bookends shape Proverbs—beginning with a father telling his son to pursue wisdom and concluding with a beautiful portrayal of an "excellent wife." Again, note the use of familial imagery.

To be sure, the book of Proverbs addresses other issues besides family. Many admonitions require individualistic application. Taming your tongue, balancing your budget, overcoming sloth, controlling your temper, cultivating generosity, and many other fruits of righteousness all rely on personal discipline and wisdom, which flow from the "fear of the Lord." But the numerous promises for family prosperity and the many admonitions for parents to raise godly children support a high estimation of the power of family to forge character. It could even be argued that individuals are more likely to pursue wisdom and godliness if those virtues were modeled for them in the early, formative days of their lives.

The "tent of the upright," contrasted with "the house of the wicked," will flourish (Prov. 14:11), have "much treasure (15:6), have rooms "filled with all precious and pleasant riches" (24:4), and serve as a "nest" from whence people should not stray (27:8).

Proverbs seems to assume that a strong marriage is the backbone of every family. Hence, the wise father presents colorful contrasts between an "excellent wife" and the other variety. The good option "is a crown of her husband" (12:4), "from the LORD" (19:14), and a source of sensual delights, capable of "intoxication" (5:19). The one who finds such a wife finds a display of God's goodness (a better understanding of that phrase than the way most translations put it—"a good thing") and "obtains favor from the LORD" (18:22). These superlatives are even more remarkable when we remember that they are "a far cry from the not uncommon ancient idea of a wife as chattel and childbearer but no companion."[5]

The wise father paints a rather different picture of the alternative. A quarrelsome wife is like a "continual dripping of rain" (19:13—an image which gets repeated in 27:15). "A desert land" is one of two locations offered as preferable to living "with a quarrelsome and fretful woman" (21:19). The other spot is "in a corner of the housetop" (21:9; 25:24).

Because God prizes family so highly, it needs protection from a variety of threats. External threats from adultery get a great deal of urgent pleading (see all the lengthy warnings in Proverbs 5–7). Internal threats that lead to strife are so

---

[5] Derek Kidner, *Proverbs: An Introduction and Commentary*, Tyndale Old Testament Commentaries (Downers Grove, IL: InterVarsity Press, 1964), 50.

bad that it would be better to have "a dry morsel with quiet than a house full of feasting with strife" (17:1).

And of course, the family is the institution in which to raise children to fear the Lord, with all the many blessings that flow from that starting point. Because "folly is bound up in the heart of a child" (22:15), parents should be "diligent" (13:24) to discipline their offspring, for that brings "hope" (19:18), "wisdom" (29:15), and "rest" (29:17). Only a fool would "despise his father's instruction" (15:5). It could even "save his soul from Sheol" (23:14).

Can people who were not raised in God-fearing homes still pursue righteousness later in life? Of course. But one has to wonder if the task is more difficult for someone with a later start. It may parallel the way an adult learning a second language has a disadvantage to a native speaker who was reared with the language permeating the walls and hearts of the home.

Satan's Plan for the Family

Given God's high ideals for what families should be— reflections of the very nature of a loving, personal God, sources of intimacy and security, and environments that foster godly character—it should come as no surprise that the Devil would want to destroy them. Or at least that he would want to mar families so they misrepresent God's character, alienate people from one another, or degenerate into hothouses for sinful behavior and thought.

It is no mere coincidence that the first ramifications from the fall were familial. The man, after being confronted by God about his sin in the garden, immediately pointed the finger at his wife as the cause of their demise: "The woman whom you gave to be with me, she gave me fruit of the tree, and I ate" (Gen. 3:12). As one preacher so poetically stated it, Adam's "bone of my bones" (see Gen. 2:23) had now become a bone of contention.

And where did the consequences of the fall next show up? In one brother's jealousy of another, eventually leading to murder. In a remarkably short number of verses, the idyllic family resort had become a satanic ground for death.

Today the Devil employs a whole host of devices to harm families. His goal is far more than making them "dysfunctional." In fact, the widespread acceptance of that term may be evidence that the Evil One has already succeeded at demeaning God's high purposes for family. Isn't "functional" a rather low goal for a family? Is that all we really want, that families "function"? Setting our goal so low and settling for merely "healing the dysfunctions" of a family, I believe, plays right into the Devil's game plan.

Instead, we should aim for families to be healthy, thriving, intimate, beautiful, strengthening, sanctifying, and, in the truest and fullest sense of the word, good. Let's declare a moratorium on the terms "dysfunctional" or "functional." Instead, let's talk of "healthy" or "unhealthy" families—especially when we talk *to* our families, no matter how "dysfunctional" they may be. Let's paint a better picture for what we want our families to be, subtly telling our parents, siblings, children, and others that we hold them in high regard. We want more for them than to be "functional"—a term better suited for cogs in gears than image-bearers sitting around our dining room tables.

Varieties of Attacks on the Family

Leo Tolstoy began his disturbing novel, *Anna Karenina*, with these puzzling words: "All happy families are alike; each unhappy family is unhappy in its own way." I think he saw that numerous weapons attack the family and cause a wide array of pain.

Since marriage serves as the foundation for the family, it follows that attacks on the family would begin at this strategic point. Spurred on by the Devil and appealing to our flesh, our world today mocks marriage, inflicting some level of insecurity into every master bedroom.

A friend recently e-mailed me with his test results related to a television special about the Ten Commandments. This show explored how well the American public was adhering to the Mosaic top ten. As you might guess, some commandments fared better than others when it came to percentage of obedience. It is comforting that the vast majority of Americans have not committed murder. It might not be surprising that over fifty percent do take the name of the Lord in vain. But my friend wrote to me after the episode about adultery. Since he had never cheated on his wife, he was rated in the highest category ("holy roller") among those who responded to the online questionnaire.

The disturbing statistic was the very high percentage of people who (voluntarily!) reported that they had committed adultery. This is not surprising however. Most movies and television shows glorify extramarital sex as better than the biblically endorsed kind. According to Hollywood, sex outside of marriage is better, more fun, and—best of all—free from negative consequences. Even when those negative consequences are admitted, they are overshadowed by such seductive, attractive portrayals of the immorality that most people find it worth the risk.

But when you talk to people who have been harmed by the sexual revolution—young men and women raised by adultery-prone parents—the images are dramatically different from the ones on TV. Young men I counsel have expressed dismay at ever being able to stay faithful to a spouse because their father failed to model such virtue. No young man should ever have to say, "My father was unfaithful to my mother," but I have heard those very words more times than I care to recount.

The sexual revolution has also yielded another, rather unanticipated fruit—sexless marriages. Dr. Phil and other marriage "experts" admit this is a trend not to be ignored. How ironic! You would have thought that our culture's end-less worship of sex would result in more, not less, actual engaging in the act.

But in a remarkably frank article in *The Atlantic Monthly*, Caitlin Flanagan addressed this phenomenon and boldly pointed to the feminist movement as a contributor to the demise of marital sex. She reviewed several books that serve as sex guides for married women to help them rediscover the joy of the marriage bed. One such book is *I Don't Know How She Does It* by Allison Pearson. Consider the level of honesty Flanagan shows here:

> If *I Don't Know How She Does It*, a book about a working woman who discovers deep joy and great sex by quitting her job and devoting herself to family life, had been written by a man, he would be the target of a lynch mob the proportions and fury of which would make Salman Rushdie feel like a lucky, lucky man. But of course it was written by a with-it female journalist, so it's safe, even admired. Allison Pearson, we have been given to understand, is telling it like it is. And what she's telling us, essentially, is that in several crucial aspects the women's move-ment has been a bust, even for the social class that most ardently championed it.[6]

The problems get worse as the model of what a family should be moves further from the biblical norm. Jesus wasn't exaggerating when he said that "the thief comes only to steal and kill and destroy . . ." (John 10:10). And Peter wasn't overstating things when he warned, "Your adversary the devil prowls around like a roaring lion, seeking someone to devour" (1 Pet. 5:8).

I need not belabor the point. The pain often associated with family seems to have no limit. Divorces, incest, and

---

[6] Caitlin Flanagan, "The Wifely Duty," *The Atlantic Monthly*, January/February 2003.

alcohol abuse, along with addictions of the widest of varieties, have made the contemporary family the exact opposite of what God intended. Perhaps Tolstoy was onto something. Normal, healthy, beautiful families *are* all alike in that they represent God and foster joy. The perversions of that goodness have more variety than we'd ever care to imagine.

Two more products of unhealthy families need consideration. Their outward displays may appear less ugly than the ones already addressed, but they cause harm and they have profound implications for the task of witnessing to family.

The first is extreme independence. The pain from divorce or abusive families propels some people toward an idolization of independence. If family didn't provide wellness, many people erect walls to protect them from further harm. They make their internal compasses their ultimate guide. Much of the self-esteem movement plays into this and hardens those who have erected such emotional fortresses. Thus, people evolve into their own god and savior. They call the shots of their lives and live out their law in remarkably religious ways. They rarely see how selfish this is but receive much societal reinforcement.

Unfortunately, the collateral damage to those around them, especially their family, is seldom considered or acknowledged. Until people see this as sin, a rebellion against the God who made them, "good news" about a Savior will seem irrelevant at best. (I'll talk more about how to break through this idol of individualism in subsequent chapters).

The second result of an unbalanced understanding of what family should be is the exact opposite of extreme individualism. It is the idolization of the family unit. Some ethnic cultures foster this kind of family or society worship more than others. In fact, it is not unfair to generalize that Western cultures tend to idolize the individual and Eastern cultures tend to idolize the group. Of course there are exceptions to this rule, but few people find themselves in places that get the balance right.

The ironic yet tragic result is that either way—whether the culture supposedly builds up the individual or devalues the individual—it's still idolatry of one form or another. And idolatry never works itself out in healthy, life-affirming ways.

For people raised in families that are a god unto themselves, hearing the gospel may seem so alien because its appeal is to individuals. How to break through this barrier will also be addressed later in this book.

Redemption for the Family

The whole point of this chapter is to help us view family from a biblical vantage point. Then our witnessing to relatives occurs in an appropriate context. How we think about our family while telling them the good news is almost as important as how we think about our message.

Family Is Not Ultimate

Despite God's high view of the family, it is important to remember that he also shows us in his Word that family is not ultimate. He alone is worthy of worship. Family must fall into place behind him.

For all the beauty, mystery, and power of marriage, Jesus taught of a balance. On the one hand, he declared, "What therefore God has joined together, let not man separate" (Mark 10:9). On the other, he revealed that in heaven, "they neither marry nor are given in marriage, but are like angels in heaven" (Matt. 22:30).

When faced with his audience's high prioritization of family, Jesus said something that must have offended some in the crowd. When he was told that his mother and his brothers were outside, Jesus asked, "Who are my mother and my brothers?" He then set a new order of relational priority by adding, "Here are my mother and my brothers! Whoever does the will of God, he is my brother and sister and mother" (see Mark 3:33–35). Apparently the ties created by a second birth hold sway over those from a first birth.

Jesus' most extreme statement about the family's place came with these words: "There is no one who has left house or brothers or sisters or mother or father or children or lands, for my sake and for the gospel, who will not receive a hundredfold now in this time, houses and brothers and sisters and mothers and children and lands, with persecutions, and in the age to come eternal life." To punctuate his statement with a timeless punch line, he adds, "But many who are first will be last, and the last first" (see Mark 10:29–31).

C. S. Lewis's thoughts about "first and second things" could apply here. He wrote of the need to keep second things second. "You can't get second things by putting them first; you can get second things only by putting first things first. From which it would follow that the question, What things are first? is of concern not only to philosophers but to everyone else."[7] Regarding family, I think Lewis would agree that when we make family more important than God or his kingdom, we distort the family and lose it. The family cannot fulfill its God-given purpose if we demand from it things which only God can provide. Such unrealistic demands from spouses, parents, children, or any other relationship cause it to be a source of pain or bitterness or alienation instead of joy, security, and intimacy.

Jesus' placing of family underneath kingdom relationships serves as both a rebuke and an encouragement. For those of us who come from healthy families, there may be a temptation to worship it or look to it for more than it can offer. Jesus' insistence to keep second things second can actually enhance an already healthy family by taking the pressure off. For those of us who did not have such a blessing, these

---

[7] C. S. Lewis, *God in the Dock* (Grand Rapids, MI: Eerdmans, 1970), 280.

words offer tremendous comfort and hope. Our newfound, gospel-crafted family, the church, can now bring wholeness, strength, sustenance, support, and maturity that we did not get from flesh and blood.

This is especially helpful for those who come from families with religious beliefs other than Christianity. Some Jewish, Muslim, Hindu, or even Buddhist families conduct a funeral for a child who places her trust in Jesus. For some, the communication lines are permanently severed.

It is also helpful to remember that Jesus himself was rejected by his own family. After selecting the Twelve "so that they might be with him and he might send them out to preach," and developing a large following of nonrelatives, those who were related to him said, "He is out of his mind" (Mark 3:14, 21). John tells us that Jesus' brothers simply "did not believe in him" (John 7:5, NIV). No wonder he summed it up with this proverb, "A prophet is not without honor except in his hometown and in his own household" (Matt. 13:57). If your earthly family doesn't listen to you or thinks you've lost your mind, remind yourself you're in good company.

Family Is Redeemable
The Bible also teaches us to not give up on even the worst of families. The gospel's power to redeem is greater than any family's depth of sin. If Paul, who rounded up Christians for arrest, persecuted the church, and gave approval to Stephen's martyrdom, could one day become "a servant of Christ Jesus" (Rom. 1:1), then so can your brother or sister or even your bisexual, dope-smoking cousin. If Peter could be transformed from a cursing denier of Jesus into a preacher to thousands on Pentecost, there's hope for your father or mother or endlessly adulterous uncle. Closer to home, if you, who once were dead in your trespasses and sins and an object of God's wrath (see Eph. 2:1–3), could be drawn to the Savior, then

so can even the most belligerent relative you have to endure every Thanksgiving.

Owen can't seem to tell his family's story without using the word "sweet" every three or four minutes. But things weren't always so sweet. His parents were separated more times than he can count while he was growing up, and they finally divorced when he was only fifteen. He lived with his father, a chain-smoking alcoholic, only because his mother could not be found. She would go missing for weeks and months at a time. Before leaving for college, Owen said he hadn't seen or heard from his mother in over a year and a half. "When I fled out of state to college, I assumed my mother was dead, and I hoped my father would soon join her."

Along with his clothes and a few books, he brought his anger and pain to college with him. He certainly brought no faith. With no religious upbringing, Owen says he may have gone to church a total of six times in his life. Still, he filled out a survey taken by a campus fellowship and listened carefully as a staff worker shared the gospel with him during his first month away from home. The good news that there was a heavenly Father who loved him—enough to send his Son to die for him—and would never forsake him sounded like good news indeed. Owen became a Christian and began to be discipled by that same campus staff worker.

Among the many topics of discussion with his discipler, Owen addressed the issue of witnessing to his parents. His wise friend told him it was important for him to let his family know about his new faith as soon as possible but to do so with no agenda for preaching to them . . . yet.

This was good advice, because God had important work to do *in* Owen before doing redemptive work *through* him. "I had to come to that painful realization that I was broken just like my parents were. When I focused in on my father's escape from reality through his alcohol or my mother's walking away from me, God would point out that I, too, dull

41

my pain with escapes from reality and I have walked away from God all my life. It was only when I began to forgive my parents that they saw something different in me that was worth asking about."

Owen's "sweet" story starts with God changing his heart of anger and hurt to one of forgiveness and love. The next part tells of his sharing the gospel with his mother. In his early twenties, he nervously (he says "shakingly") read *The Four Spiritual Laws* booklet to his mother as they sat at her kitchen table. He says it was good to have such a tool to keep him on track because his nerves made it difficult for him to think straight. At forty-four years of age, Owen's mother trusted Christ for salvation and restoration. The same scenario played out between Owen and his father less than a year later. Same result. One year after that, his parents began a lengthy (and presumably messy) process of reconciliation with each other. A short time later, they restated their marriage vows before a tear-filled family gathering—in a church.

The gospel bore fruit in Owen's sister's and brother's lives as well. It also provided strength in other ways. His parents enjoyed a Christ-centered marriage in a gospel-centered church for a full decade, during which time his Mom developed into quite the initiative-taking evangelist. Who knows how many came to the Savior as a by-product of that nerve-racked, booklet-reading college student's conversation with his mother.

But then bad news invaded the garden and Owen's Dad was diagnosed with cancer and a few other diseases. Each one, perhaps, would not have been fatal, but the cumulative effect eventually took his life. Their entire family's faith gave them strength to handle this trial—Owen's Dad had assurance of salvation, his Mom had hope in the midst of horrendous pain, and Owen marveled at a God who loved them all.

If you were to ask Owen today about how to witness to your family, he would say it's all about grace, truth, and love.

"I had to see the grace of God toward me before I could see it extend to them. I had to be honest about the pain I felt, while remembering what pain I caused Jesus on the cross. And I had to experience God's love before I tried to share it."

Implications for Evangelism

So how does knowing God's view of our family help us share the gospel with them? Two implications must be mentioned. The first is that evangelizing family is difficult.

M. Scott Peck began his bestselling book, *The Road Less Traveled,* with these words:

> Life is difficult. This is a great truth, one of the greatest truths. (The first of the "Four Noble Truths" which Buddha taught was "life is suffering.") It is a great truth because once we truly see this truth, we transcend it. Once we truly know that life is difficult—once we truly understand and accept it—then life is no longer difficult. Because once it is accepted, the fact that life is difficult no long matters.[8]

I quote this for three reasons. First, I think Peck is onto something—accepting that life is difficult can be a transformative experience that can be very helpful. But second, I think Peck goes too far. While I agree with the first part of his statement, I think he is naïve to think that this takes away the difficulty. And to add that, "once it is accepted, the fact that life is difficult no long matters" is just plain foolish. Third, I think many Christians have accepted this kind of Buddhist frame of reference for some aspects of their lives, including evangelism. But this worldview gets them into trouble because it is contrary to Scripture.

I do believe that life is difficult, and I also believe that evangelism is difficult, and I especially believe that evangelizing family members is very difficult. But just realizing

---

[8] M. Scott Peck, *The Road Less Traveled* (New York: Touchstone, 1978), 15.

that does not reduce the difficulty. It only helps us tackle a problem with the depth of effort it needs. When you know the difficulty of running a marathon, you train for it, eat the right foods, get proper rest, etc. If you think it's going to be easy, you'll probably drop out of the race early on. And indeed many Christians do drop out of the race of witnessing (to family or anyone else) because they thought it was going to be easy.

They had good reason for thinking this, by the way. Many books and seminars train people to witness using terms like "simple," or "natural," or "everyday" to describe a task, which turns out to be "difficult" or "frustrating" or "painful."

I even saw this sales pitch in a catalog of Christian books for an evangelism primer: "This book shows you how easy and natural evangelism can be. It tells you the three questions to ask, the two illustrations to use, and the only Bible verse you'll ever need in any situation." I am encouraged that newer books admit the immensity of the task right in their title. I am thinking of books like *Evangelism for the Rest of Us*, *Evangelism for the Tongue-Tied*, and *Evangelism Made Slightly Less Difficult.*[9]

Peck is right that we must recognize that life, or some parts of it, are difficult. He is surely wrong to say what he says next. Instead, we, as Christians, should view life through biblical lenses rather than Buddhist ones. When we do, we'll see that our world is fallen, people are slaves to sin, we don't have sufficient compassion for the lost, and the Devil is not sitting idly by as we tell people to turn from darkness into the light of Christ.

In other words, our goal, whether talking to family members or anyone else, should not be for "comfortable evange-

---

[9] Mike Bechtle, *Evangelism for the Rest of Us* (Grand Rapids, MI: Baker, 2006); Chap Bettis, *Evangelism for the Tongue-Tied* (Enumclaw, WA: Winepress, 2004); Nick Pollard, *Evangelism Made Slightly Less Difficult* (Downers Grove, IL: InterVarsity Press, 1997).

lism" or "natural evangelism" or "easy evangelism," but rather evangelism that heralds accurately and powerfully the goodness of the gospel—regardless of the difficulty for us in proclaiming it or the resistance from those who hear it.

A second implication is that evangelizing family is probably going to be more emotionally charged than witnessing to strangers or other acquaintances. Two emotional struggles need to be highlighted—guilt and anger. Both seem to attack from within and without.

We feel guilt from within because we think we're not being bold enough or effective enough or patient enough or loving enough or clear enough with our witness. There may or may not be any substance to this. In other words, this may be false guilt. But some of us have real guilt because of the ways we've acted in the past. Our family, in other words, has seen us at our worst, and the guilt we feel for losing our temper or any other display of sin immobilizes us in our witness. "How can I tell my brother about Christ if I'm such a bad example of Christian living?" we wonder.

Some of us feel guilt coming from the outside—from our relatives—because they view us as a traitor to our family or, in some cases, our entire race. Jewish, Muslim, and Hindu converts to the Christian faith face this sometimes more intently than people coming from other faith traditions.

Padma's father was a Hindu priest who responded to his daughter's salvation testimony by yelling, "If you ever walk into a church again, I will kill myself." I don't know if I recommend Padma's response as a universal prescription for all who may find themselves in this kind of situation, but her reply was, "Oh, no you won't. Stop being so dramatic."

It would take an entire book to address the topic of guilt sufficiently but a shorthand plan for handling guilt must begin with distinguishing between true and false guilt. If the guilt is a form of baseless condemnation, we need to "take every thought captive" (take control over the thought instead of allowing it to control us), examine its content, call the accusation a lie if that is indeed what it is, and answer it with the truth. This takes a level of internal dialogue that may require practice but it is well worth the effort.[10]

In the case of accusations of true guilt (you really did lose your temper, acted like a jerk, got drunk, used "unwholesome" vocabulary, laughed at a dirty joke, told a dirty joke, etc.), the response must be the gospel. "Preaching the gospel to yourself" is an essential lifelong, transformational skill.

We need to resist the temptation to respond to accusations of guilt (whether from within or without) with antidotes other than the cross. We must not offer up accounts of virtue that might counterbalance our sin or present pledges for better performance in the future. Instead, we must confess with statements like this: "Yes. You're right. I was wrong to lose my temper." In some settings, you could add, "I guess that's why I need forgiveness from you and from God."

Regarding the false guilt that comes from our relatives—attacks for being a traitor, etc.—a simple piece of advice I would offer is, "Don't fall for it." Guilt manipulation, whether it's the Jewish, Muslim, Hindu, Catholic, or any other version, must be disarmed by disengagement. For some, this disarming will be a brand new experience. Once again, the key is the gospel. Now that you have come to faith in Christ, you must saturate your thinking with the grandest diffuser of guilt: "There is therefore now no condemnation for those who are in Christ Jesus" (Rom. 8:1).

When parents try to manipulate their adult children with guilt (which probably has worked hundreds of times before), it is crucial for the adult child to break that cycle with a calm, loving expression of nonengagement. This may take practice. Here are some gracious things you could try to say, if you ever face a situation like Padma's:

---

[10] A helpful resource to help with this process is Timothy S. Lane and Paul David Tripp, *How People Change* (Greensboro, NC: New Growth Press, 2006).

"No, Dad. I don't think you'll kill yourself. I certainly would not want you to. But I will continue to explore my faith. And that will involve my going to church."

"Our family has always valued respect for one another, haven't we? I'm simply asking you to respect my decisions. I'll never express my religious opinions in disrespectful ways. And, if I do, you can call me on it."

"I need to ask you to treat me like an adult. I've made some decisions that I'm sure you don't like. But I'd like to talk about faith issues calmly. Maybe now is not the best time to try that."

Another emotional component that needs some forethought is anger.[11] Like guilt, this can come from within and from without. Sometimes we get angry at our family (for not understanding us, for not understanding the gospel, for getting angry at us, for using sarcasm or guilt manipulation toward us, etc.). Sometimes they get angry at us, and we need to know how to respond.

An important key in diffusing anger, wherever it comes from, is to preach the gospel to yourself—often enough and thoroughly enough that patience, grace, and love flow out rather than insults, wrath, and lava. I will address this more in the next chapter. For now, it may suffice to ask how would your response to anger change if you meditated on one of these statements:

"I'd probably react with anger too, if one of my relatives were telling me I've been wrong about religion my whole life. The only reason I see things differently now is the grace of God. I can ask him to give me patience in this situation."

---

[11] I devote an entire chapter on anger and how it relates to evangelism in my book, *Questioning Evangelism: Questioning People's Hearts the Way Jesus Did* (Grand Rapids, MI: Kregel, 2004).

"I'm probably angry at my father (or whoever) right now because I want him to submit to me. In fact, I *need* him to submit to me because I worship control. Control is my idol. No wonder I need a Savior. I worship false gods. Thank you for the gospel's cleansing of my idolatry."

"She's angry at me. Her anger is making me angry back at her. But, then again, my sin made God angry at me . . . and he chose to pour out his anger on his Son instead of on me. May that kind of love flow from him through me to her."

These are not naturally occurring thoughts for most of us. But once we start rehearsing them in our minds (part of what Paul called, "the renewal of your mind" in Rom. 12:2), they start to inspire similar thought. Learning this new language can be a beautiful and transformative experience—even if it takes time and effort.

We could go on, looking at a whole host of other emotional issues. For some, it would be beneficial to thoroughly study, through the lens of Scripture, specific issues that trip you up—fear, anxiety, shame, loss, sadness, etc. I encourage you to shine the light of God's Word on these potential landmines.[12] This may involve hard work, but it will pay huge dividends toward the goal of sharing Christ with your family. It is unlikely that you'll make much headway if you just focus on evangelism techniques while ignoring the background noise of emotional stress.

Several people I spoke to expressed frustration from lack of objectivity. This seems to be in short supply when we're around our family. "I'm otherwise a rational and calm person," Molly told me over a cup of coffee, "but when I get around my family, I lose all sense of composure and objectivity."

---

[12] My favorite source for help on emotions is the Christian Counseling and Education Foundation. See www.ccef.org.

But maybe objectivity is the wrong goal—or, at least, an unrealistic one. Maybe the strong ties of family, woven into the relationships by God, make total objectivity impossible. Maybe we should aim for (and pray for) other goals. The problem with objectivity is that it seems to require a stoic, dispassionate detachment. Often this comes across as uncaring or apathetic. That would be the last thing we would want to communicate to people we love as we proclaim a message of God's love. In other words, perhaps the goal of love is better than a goal of objectivity. When we stand in love (flowing from God to us through Christ) and show forth love (in words and with actions), we can let go of the anger, disengage the guilt, and share the gospel so that it truly sounds like gracious, attractive good news instead of haughty, condemning bad news.

Steps to Take

1. If you don't already have one, develop a system for prayer for your family. Perhaps you can set aside a section in a prayer journal. Or maybe you can insert photos of your family members in a place where you look for prayer prompters.

2. Begin your prayers for your family with thanksgiving. This may be more difficult for some people than others. Regardless of your family's well-being, thank God for the family you have and all the accompanying benefits you can identify. Thank God for his love for each family member and all the gifts he's given them.

3. You may need to include prayers of confession as well—confession of your lack of love for your family, your idolatry of control in trying to change them, your reliance on your ability to convict them of their sin instead of trusting the Holy Spirit to do that, your coldheartedness, haughtiness, and self-righteousness,

etc. Ask the Holy Spirit to shine his light of truth on your darkness of sin.

4. If you haven't already done so, "come out of the closet" as a Christian to your family. Pray for gentle words and a gracious demeanor mixed with bold confidence. Decide who would be the safest person to tell first. (I do not advise a group announcement at a holiday dinner table!) Aim for your announcement to be informational rather than evangelistic. You can trust God to open evangelistic doors later. For now, it's time to couch things in sentences like this: "Mom, there's something I think you should know about me. I've come to the place where I've decided to embrace Christianity as my faith." Or, "Dad, I've become a Christian and it's beginning to have some good effects in my life. It's all rather new, but I thought I'd tell you early on, just so you'd know what's going on."

GRACE

Amazing and Yet Breaking

When I told people I was writing a book on witnessing to family, I starting hearing tougher stories than I had bargained for.

George's brother Mark has been in a drug-saturated cult for almost a decade and has pretty much lost his mind from the peyote, ecstasy, and LSD. As a result of the cult's illegal activities, Mark is now hunted by law enforcement authorities in several states. So George only hears from Mark when it might be safe for him to send e-mail using one of a host of aliases.

I've heard George talk about his brother many times. I don't think it's ever without tears and desperate pleas for prayer. "How can I break the gospel through to someone whose mind is blown away by drugs?" he asked me.

Paul has not spoken to his brother Leo in almost a decade, because when they last saw each other, Leo threatened Paul's life. Partly because of a genetic mental illness and partly from Leo's New Age chanting, the two are as far apart as brothers could be. But their father is getting close to death. "Can two

51

guys serve as pallbearers without ever talking to each other?" he wonders.

Alison came to faith as a freshman in college. Soon thereafter she changed her position on abortion from "pro-choice" to "pro-life." This seemed only natural to her new friends in the campus fellowship. But it sounded like treason to Alison's mother, a national leader in the abortion rights movement. While Alison marched in Washington with a placard that read "Stop Abortion Now," her mother stood a few hundred yards away chanting, "Keep your rosaries off my ovaries." Alison asked me (without the slightest hint of sarcasm), "Would you be willing to come to my house this Thanksgiving and tell my Mom about Psalm 139?"

Jacob grew up attending a church that spoke more about social issues than salvation. He never heard the gospel until he went off to college. When he trusted Christ in the fall semester of his freshman year, he couldn't wait to tell his father (and his father's second wife) and his mother (and her fourth husband) and his eleven (Or was it twelve? He wasn't sure.) stepbrothers and stepsisters.

He found the New Testament's teaching on sexual purity especially helpful since his parents' numerous marriages have been plagued with infidelity. Jacob's newfound faith has created only a minor strain in his relationship with his parents, but his newfound morality has forged a major rift. It seems he gets more ridicule for *not* sleeping with his girlfriend from his sexually "liberated" parents (and the cast of replacement spouses) than he does from his fraternity brothers. "How do I reach them?" he asked me with a tone of voice that blended pain and anger.

And these are just people I know. I started noticing even more dramatic stories in newspapers—stories of Muslim converts to Christianity whose families plan to murder them, and homeschooled Christian children whose relatives fear they've entered a cult and seek legal action to force them into public schools, and other similarly bizarre nightmares.

In addition to the qualifiers stating I have changed people's names and their stories' details, I wondered if I also needed to state:

Warning: I have training in theology and experience in ministry but no background in psychology, pathology, jurisprudence, law enforcement, cult extraction, deprogramming, or exorcism.

I stopped marshaling defensive statements when I realized that while there are significant limits to this book, there are no limits to God's grace. Realistically, there could have been some cousin of the apostle Paul sitting around some prayer meeting centuries ago telling his fellow believers, "Hey, would you guys pray for my cousin Saul? I can't think of anyone more lost. He hunts down followers of The Way and arrests them. Just last week, he was the guy who stood guard over the clothes of the people who killed our brother Stephen."

All this leads me to say that the process of witnessing to family needs to begin in our hearts. For us to have fruitful outreach to our family, we need a wellspring of grace flowing from within. This chapter seeks to jumpstart that process by stimulating your amazement at the wonder of grace.

I gained some appreciation for grace in an unlikely place— the hospital. An anesthesiologist was about to stick a needle into my spine. You know how doctors love to ask probing (pun intended) questions as they're about to do something that will surely hurt. They call it "speech anesthesia." If they can get you talking about what you do for a living or your kid's baseball team or politics or last night's episode of *Dancing with the Stars*, they think the incision by the scalpel or the injection of the needle won't hurt. I have never found this to be effective.

Dr. Leonard tried this speech anesthesia as he attempted to alleviate pain in my lower back due to a herniated disc. I was to receive epidural injections as a three-dose series over the course of a month. Injection number one came at the beginning of the month, with each succeeding dose coming two weeks apart. By the end of three shots after four weeks, I was supposed to be pain free.

So Dr. Leonard asked me what I do for a living as he "prepared the site" for his first sticking. I told him I was in campus ministry.

Two weeks later, at the moment of invasion of injection number two, he asked what denomination I was.

When injection number three came along, Dr. Leonard was still intent on talking about religion. I got the idea he assumed, by now, that after successfully weathering two prior injections, I would be calm and able to concentrate on serious conversation. Nothing could have been further from the truth.

Still, he asked what I thought about "ridiculous religious fanatics" who believe you go to hell if you dance or smoke or drink. He had gone to a church full of such people when he was in high school and had heard more about hellfire than he had ever heard before.

"What do you think about that, Mr. Newman? Do you think people go to hell if they dance or smoke or drink? What do you believe about Jesus?"

I'll tell you exactly what I was thinking at that point in time. I thought, "Not now! I don't want to have a witnessing opportunity now! I don't want to talk *about* Jesus. I want to talk *to* Jesus: 'Oh, Jesus, don't let me die!'"

That's not what I said, of course. What I was able to squeak out was something like, "I'd really like to talk about this. But right now, I'm a little preoccupied."

"Oh. Sure. No problem," he said, almost as if I had reminded him of what he should be concentrating on—my spine!

When he finished a few minutes later, he returned to his question. I could tell he was very curious about my beliefs. After all, this line of questioning no longer served as speech anesthesia. He restated his question with a tone of seriousness that let me know I needed to answer him thoughtfully.

"What do you think about all those rules?" he asked. "Don't dance. Don't drink. Don't smoke. Is that how people get into heaven?"

How would you have answered him? I promise I'll tell you what I said at the end of this chapter. But before I do, a little reflection about the nature of our message could encourage us to hold out hope for even the most unlikely candidates for sainthood—even members of our own families. As I reflect on the nature of grace, as the Bible depicts it, I am struck by three realities: Grace is available. Grace is an offense. And grace is amazing.

Grace Is Available

People often study the contrasts between Paul's preaching in Jewish settings like Pisidian Antioch (recorded in Acts 13) and his message in Athens before a non-Jewish, nonspiritual crowd (recorded in Acts 17). Such a study provides great insight for reaching our far-from-the-gospel world today. I'll look at some of the lessons I've learned along those lines in the next chapter.

But we dare not skip the record of Paul's ministry in Lystra, where he faced another kind of audience. Unlike the biblically literate Jewish group in the synagogue or the secular philosophers on Mars Hill, Lystra afforded Paul the opportunity to tailor his appeal to worshipers of Greek gods. In other words, these were not irreligious people like those in Athens, but they were not religious Jews like those in Pisidia. Their religion was based on something other than the Bible. Like many people today, the people in Lystra might have described themselves as "spiritual but not religious."

Paul's message went in directions we might not have anticipated. When the people interpreted Paul and Barnabas's healing powers by saying, "The gods have come down to us in the likeness of men!" (Acts 14:11), they concluded that Paul was Hermes and Barnabas was Zeus. (Isn't it amazing how some people's responses to the gospel are bizarre! They'd sooner believe nonsense than the truth.)

After rebuking the people for worshiping "men, of like nature with you," Paul offered this "good news": "you should turn from these vain things to a living God, who made the heaven and the earth and the sea and all that is in them. In past generations he allowed the nations to walk in their own ways. Yet he did not leave himself without witness, for he did good by giving you rains from heaven and fruitful seasons, satisfying your hearts with food and gladness" (Acts 14:15–17).

Certain aspects of this minisermon do not surprise us. The call to repentance, the pointing to God as Creator, and the contrast of a "living God" to "vain things" all appear frequently in modern-day evangelistic tools. But it is Paul's appeal to God's goodness that deserves careful attention and application today.

Paul speaks of God leaving a witness for himself in things like rain, seasons, food, and gladness. He says to unsaved pagans that they can look at the fruitful world around them and the full bellies within them and find evidence of a good God. (I am especially taken by the notion that food can serve as a pre-evangelistic device.) What a contrast to many of our efforts to first convince people how miserable they are. Paul made sure to point to how happy they were!

I would hate to count how many of my attempts to start with misery-based apologetics have failed to produce repentance and conversion. Those conversations may have sounded this bad:

Me: "Aren't you empty inside?"

Them: "Not really."

Me: "Aren't you looking for more out of life?"

Them: "More what? More money? Sure. More happiness? Of course. More fun? Why not?"

Me: "Pascal said we all have a God-shaped vacuum inside us. Can you relate to that?"

Them: "Pascal who?"

Me: "Aren't you miserable without Jesus?"

Them: "Only if you keep talking to me about him."

Why not start with joy-based apologetics instead? Why not talk to people about the good things in life that we enjoy so much—food, friends, beauty, etc., and try to see if we can point them to the Giver of such good gifts? The fact that Paul included "rain" in his presentation might very well be an allusion to the many places in the Old Testament where rain was a sign of God's gracious provision (see Ps. 147:8; Isa. 30:23) and to Jesus' teaching in the Sermon on the Mount (Matt. 5:45).

Please note. I am not saying we should *substitute* such nonnegotiables as sin, judgment, and repentance with what I am calling joy-based apologetics. After all, Paul began his gospel presentation in Lystra with a call to "turn from worthless things" (Acts 14:15, NIV). I am saying that God's goodness should also find its way into our evangelism.

It did for Jesus. Remember how he carefully wove together conviction-based apologetics with the joy-based variety when he initiated his culture-clashing conversation with a Samaritan woman at a well? He pointed in a positive direction. He spoke of "living water . . . that will become . . . a spring of water welling up to eternal life" (see John 4:10–15). But once she became intrigued enough to pursue such an appealing gift, he brought in some information about her marriages and morality that were less welcome. If there's one thing we must learn from Jesus' examples of evangelism, it's that there isn't just one thing for us to learn. There are many lessons, many approaches, and many ways to clarify the one way of salvation. Different audiences require different methods. An appeal to goodness is one way we should reach out, especially when witnessing to family. They are the very people with whom we may have shared these displays of God's goodness.

Traditionally, Christians have affirmed this doctrine and called it "common grace." This grace is available to all and, in fact, benefits all whether they acknowledge it or not. In this way, common grace is different from the specific grace of the cross, which only benefits those who bow before it, acknowledge their need for it, and appropriate it by faith. My point (and I think it was Paul's as well) is that in some situations, starting with common grace can pave the way to openness toward the specific grace of the gospel.

Ray, a retired Navy officer, told me that his many attempts to witness to his unsaved sister never amounted to anything until he stopped criticizing her expensive tastes in decorating and lavish style of entertaining. "Her Thanksgiving dinners were so extravagant, all I could think of was how much money could have gone to missions instead. I ruined many family meals by talking about starving people who would be so much better off if we just sacrificed some more."

At some point, he experimented with a different tactic. He started asking about the paintings on his sister's walls and the color choices of paint. He even started helping out in the kitchen and spoke of the joy of cooking. Although they approached it from differing perspectives, Ray and his sister enjoyed God's bounty as something worth celebrating. Only then did some avenues for spiritual conversations begin to open up.

Not only do we need to preach the gospel to ourselves, we need to preach the doctrine of common grace to ourselves. We need to remind our pride-prone souls that everything, not just Jesus' death on the cross on our behalf, is a gift. Every breath, every step, every meal, every prompter of joy, comes from a God who has not left himself without a witness. Paul's rhetorical question to the Corinthians, "What do you have that you did not receive? . . ." (1 Cor. 4:7) should tune our hearts toward gratitude and humility. If that happens, our efforts to reach out to family will sound more like good news than like another nagging.

Grace Is an Outrage

Let's not be naïve. Although grace is common, it can also sting. Our merit-based economies and resume-building selves don't sit well with unmerited favor. Maybe we want some level of forgiveness from God. That just seems reasonable. But total forgiveness based on an innocent Savior's atonement? Well, that seems to go too far.

Grace, as revealed in the Scriptures, should shock us. Whether it is from the mouth of a prophet or the Messiah himself, the message of grace feels a bit like a punch in the stomach that requires some recovery time.

Ezekiel told a graphic story of an abandoned baby girl who was rescued from certain death, cared for, provided for, and eventually brought into the rescuer's home as a beloved wife. (See if you can read Ezekiel 16 without shedding tears!) Then, as if to spit in the face of her beloved husband, this woman sinned beyond belief. Listen to Ezekiel's damning recounting of the story: "You trusted in your beauty and played the whore because of your renown and lavished your whorings on any passerby; your beauty became his. You took some of your garments and made for yourself colorful shrines, and on them played the whore. The like has never been, nor ever shall be" (Ezek. 16:15–16).

But this is not the most shocking part of the prophet's words. After sparing no detail of Israel's "whoredom," he pronounces, "For thus says the Lord GOD: I will deal with you as you have done, you who have despised the oath in bringing the covenant, yet I will remember my covenant with you in the days of your youth, and I will establish for you an everlasting covenant." He says he will do all this so that "you will remember your ways and be ashamed . . . and you shall know that I am the LORD, that you may remember and be confounded . . . when I atone for you for all that you have done, declares the Lord GOD" (Ezek. 16:59–63).

Don't miss the word "confounded." Grace is a scandal, an outrage. When grace no longer confounds, it no longer transforms.

This is exactly why Jesus told his threefold parable of the lost sheep, lost coin, and lost son. The lost sheep and lost coin stories were a set up to make us expect a happy ending for the third story. The lost sheep was found and there was a party. The lost coin was found and another celebration ensued. When the lost son was found and there was much rejoicing, we expect Jesus to end the story on a happy note. But he didn't (and we dare not quit reading the parable at that point). This shouldn't surprise us. After all, he began the third part of the parable with the words, "There was a man who had two sons" (Luke 15:11).[1] If we think the story is only about the so-called prodigal son, we have missed a key element foreshadowed in the opening line.

For our purposes, it is worth reflecting on Jesus' use of a family setting to tell this parable. He could have used other relational ties like the king-servant or landowner-worker, as he did in other parables. But to make the strongest impact, he chose to contrast the outrage of grace with the ugliness of self-righteousness in the family realm. It is a father's love for his two sons and the elder brother's resentment of it that illustrate the core of this lesson. Home may be "where the

---

[1] See Timothy Keller's *The Prodigal God* (New York: Dutton, 2008) for an excellent, extended reflection on this parable and an appreciation of God's grace in the face of our self-righteousness.

heart is," but it's also where we let the darkness of those hearts display themselves for all to see.

While the immensity of the father's love for the younger brother certainly moves us, it is not the main point of the story. Yes, we marvel at the father's running toward his returning son, the lavish provision of a robe, ring, shoes, and fattened calf. But Jesus told the story to disturb rather than delight.

Several speeches punctuate this parable. The younger brother begins the drama with a short speech that basically says, "Give me my money." He prepares a second speech of confession while wallowing in the mud. He only gets to deliver two-thirds of that speech ("I've sinned. . . . I am no longer worthy. . . .") because he gets interrupted before he can ask to be treated as one of his father's hired servants. The father's speech reveals that there is no such second-class citizenship in his home, and he climaxes his pronouncement of grace with, "For this my son was dead, and is alive again; he was lost, and is found . . ." (Luke 15:24). He will say these words again in a private speech to his older son as the punch line at the end of the parable.

But it is the next speech that voices what many of us would say if we were honest. "Where's my party!"[2] we demand, revealing our own version of "elder brother syndrome." The whining older brother contrasts the truly prodigal father. ("Prodigal" means "lavish." The father was overly generous.) "Look, these many years I have served you, and I never disobeyed your command, yet you never gave me a young goat, that I might celebrate with my friends. But when this son of yours came, who has devoured your property with prostitutes, you killed the fattened calf for him!" (Luke 15:29–30).

Part of the reason grace bothers us so much is because self-righteousness distorts our perception of reality. We see

---

[2] See the excellent article by Mark Buchanan, "Where's *My* Party?" *Discipleship Journal* (September/October 2004), http://www.navpress.com/magazines/archives/article.aspx?id=10166.

our goodness as far better than it really is, and we see others' sins as worse than they really are. In the midst of such unclear vision, grace makes no sense at all.

The older brother claims to have "never" disobeyed the father. Really? As a father, I find that hard to believe. He says that his father "never" gave him a young goat (or, by implication, any other gracious gifts). Really? As a son who has received gift upon gift from my earthly father, I find that equally hard to believe. The older brother even disowns any kinship with the returning prodigal by calling him "this son of yours." (The father doesn't let him get away with it, however, and gently refers to him as "this, your brother.")

The older brother even embellishes the story by adding that his despised sibling got involved "with prostitutes." How could he know such detail? Perhaps word got back home of such lewdness. But I wonder if it's more likely that self-righteousness so distorts our reasoning that we're willing to lie about others' behavior to make ours look better.

The father is equally gracious to both sons because both were lost. One was lost in licentiousness. The other was lost in self-righteousness. The father displayed equal grace by running to one son and coming outside the party to the other son. (By the way, we don't hear how the older brother responded. The curtain goes down on this drama with the elder brother still outside.)

The parable was prompted by the Pharisees' grumbling words about Jesus because he "receives sinners and eats with them" (Luke 15:2). The point of the parable provides the antidote—grace. Nothing else will do. Self-righteousness or any other hyphenated term that begins with "self" can never produce salvation. Grace alone will heal while it wounds. It is only when we are first outraged by God's complete forgiveness that we can then bask in it.

As we bring the gospel home to our family, we dare not do so as a self-righteous older brother. Even if our family members are out squandering their inheritance with prostitutes or wallowing in the mud with pigs, if we're pointing to our record of good behavior while condemning their wicked ways, it will be some message other than the gospel that they hear. They would be wise to reject such a message.

Grace Is Amazing

When Peter began his first epistle, he rehearsed a deep reflection on the wonder of grace. He spoke of God's "great mercy" and our "being "born again to a living hope." He described our gospel inheritance with the adjectives "imperishable, undefiled, and unfading." And he marveled that this truth was so profound that it would prompt rejoicing even while undergoing great trials (see 1 Pet. 1:3–7).

Peter's words should affect both our hearts and our minds. He tells us, "Though you have not seen him, you love him. Though you do not now see him, you believe in him and rejoice with joy that is inexpressible and filled with glory . . ." (vv. 8–9). After a bit more reflection that challenges our intellect and delights our soul, he says that these are "things into which angels long to look" (v. 12).

The gospel is so good, so rich, so awe-inspiring that even angels, beings that have been around a very long time and have had the privilege of sitting in the front row to watch quite a few of God's miraculous acts, say they'd like to investigate further.

Somehow we've tamed this message so that our response is somewhat less enthusiastic. Often the way we think about and proclaim the gospel elicits a nod that indicates nothing more than, "that makes sense." We need to find ways to preach the good news (both to ourselves and to others) in ways that cause wonder and amazement.

This begins with more emphasis on how bad we are. Only then can we appreciate how good God's grace is.

Perhaps a young teacher's experiment can shed some light on this. I have heard New Testament scholar D. A. Carson tell this story and have found it to be helpful. He knew a young woman who taught religion to middle-school boys in a part of Ireland that wasn't known for its godliness. These boys were rough, and this young woman had her work cut out for her. Her curriculum called for lessons on the first few chapters from Genesis.

Chapter 1 didn't go well. The boys paid little attention to her lofty lectures about God's creative acts. Chapter 2 only got a little more response because the boys snickered at the thought that the man and woman in the garden were naked.

How could she speak of the intricacies of Genesis 3? Nothing could be more important for these boys to grasp than the reality of the fall. If ever there were people who needed to know God viewed them as rebels, it was these young hooligans.

She opted for a bold experiment. The day after the lesson on chapter 2, she dressed in less than fine clothes and said they were going to have a playday with modeling clay and papier-mâché. "Today we're going to create a world," she told them. "We're going to use these things to make our own little planet, and tomorrow we'll make creatures to put on our planet." The boys responded with much joy!

As you might guess, middle-school boys chose to inhabit their newly created planet with creatures that all looked like Godzilla, fire-breathing dragons, and sharp-toothed goblins. For several days they "played" with their creatures on their planet and had a grand old time.

Then one day the teacher announced: "We need some rules for your creatures. They're biting each others' heads off, falling into the water and melting (remember that they were made of clay and papier-mâché), and ruining the planet." So the boys put together a list of rules, one of the first being, "You must obey us, your creators!"

After a day or two of playing by the rules (or else experiencing the dragon equivalent of a timeout), the young teacher began a class with another announcement: "The creatures have decided not to obey your rules."

Middle-school boys are not known for their subtlety. "What?" they cried.

"They're not going to obey your rules. They told me. They've got free will. They don't like your restrictive rules. Now, go play with them. But remember that they're not going to do what you say."

One by one, the boys expressed outrage.

"But we made them!" they insisted.

"So what?" she replied.

Finally, one boy from the back of the room stood up, hands on hips, and yelled at the top of his lungs, "I'll break their #^@* legs!"

Now she knew they were ready to study Genesis 3.

Until our rebellion against our Creator is seen as horrific as it really is, God's rescue out of that mess won't seem all that great. But if we can find ways to drive home the audacity of our sin, the sheer gall of creatures telling their creator to buzz off (or worse!), we could set our listeners up to marvel that this same Creator chose to be our Redeemer as well.

It is only when we grasp that God is both "just" (he has every right to wipe us off the face of the earth) and "the justifier" (he takes our punishment upon himself), that we could rightly respond with a few hundred choruses of "Amazing Grace" (see Rom. 3:26).

Implications for Evangelism

First, if common grace is something that all people experience, let's point it out to them. And let's be sure to use the pronouns "we" and "us" far more than "you." So often our evangelism takes on an ugly "you vs. me" tone ("You're a sinner. I'm forgiven." "You're lost. I'm found."). Common grace should mitigate that. Let's find ways to talk about what "we" have in common that point us to the Giver of all gifts. We'll have ample opportunity to point out our differences later on.

When I was a new Christian, spending more and more time with people who had grown up in the faith, I felt as if I were immersed in a new community that spoke a foreign language. It was the language of praise. I'm not just talking about how they spoke about God ("Oh, praise the Lord!"). I'm referring to how these people expressed gratitude and appreciation for God's many blessings. ("Isn't this a blessing for all of us to be together around this dinner table?" "Hasn't God been good to us in keeping us all in good health?" "Isn't it amazing how God made so many delicious varieties of fruit?") Considering the negative environment in which I grew up and the fluency with which I spoke sarcasm and cynicism, I thought these people were the biggest phonies on the planet. But something about them kept drawing me toward them and I found that they were not fake at all. Although this language was foreign to my ears, it was beautiful and I longed to learn it.

Our world continues to devolve into cynicism. Song lyrics moan, "I don't care that you don't care." Television sitcoms consist almost entirely of put-downs and forms of despair. At first these "jokes" may make us laugh. But eventually, we soak in a negativity that eats away at us.

As messengers of the gospel, we can sound different— and ask God to use our appreciation of his common grace to attract people to himself. The image of God within them could resonate with our praise. Then, we can transition from expressions of gratitude for God's good gifts to the gospel with statements like these:

"I'm learning to get to know the God who gives us such beauty."

"Slowly but surely, I'm finding where these good gifts come from."

"Do you ever wonder who's behind all this goodness?"

For some, this kind of conversation may be rather unnatural. In family situations especially, we tend to devolve to former manners of speech, much of which were sarcastic, insincere, and negative. But once you learn this new dialect, you will find its beauty well worth the effort to express. After a while, your family will stop looking at you with puzzled looks and may even join you in the newfound language.

Perhaps this is too direct for some families. In many cases, we would do well to talk about God's goodness and grace from an angle. The direct light of God's brilliance may blind people, as Emily Dickinson warned in her short poem, "*Tell It Slant*":

> Tell all the truth but tell it slant
> Success in circuit lies
> Too bright for our infirmed delight
> The truth's superb surprise.
> As lightning to the children eased
> With explanation kind,
> The truth must dazzle gradually
> Or every man be blind.[3]

If your family has a long history of negativity and sarcasm, the intermediate step of speaking positively about a good meal or a great film may pave the way for "blinding" talk of God's grace and mercy. The gradual approach may prove more effective than the dump truck method (see chap. 6 on time).

---

[3] Emily Dickinson, "Tell It Slant," in *The Norton Anthology of Poetry* (New York: Norton), 855.

In short, the doctrine of common grace should influence our evangelism so that we talk about the goodness of the gospel, not just its truth. So many books and seminars on apologetics give weight to the truth of our message. I do not want to minimize that at all. But our message needs to sound like *good* news, not just true facts.

Second, if grace is an outrage, we should share our testimony with wonder rather than pride. For some Christians, their sharing of the gospel sounds like, "I once was stupid, but now I'm smart. I once was bad, but now I've cleaned up my act." This is far from the sentiment of John Newton's, "I once was blind, but now I see." We need to rid all our outreach attempts of any credit we might take or intelligence we might express. We didn't become Christians because we're smarter than our relatives or anyone else. We didn't get saved by earning it. Still, I have heard too many people make statements like, "I'm so glad I had the good sense to accept Christ" or "I couldn't deny the truthfulness of the gospel. I can't understand why my brother is so stubborn."

This is hard to remember because once we are reborn, God does indeed start a transformation process that gives us "the mind of Christ" and new eyes to see and a newly softened heart. We are most certainly "new creations" (see 2 Cor. 5:17).

Perhaps C. S. Lewis's insight may help us maintain the biblical balance here: "The Christian has a great advantage over other men, not by being less fallen than they nor less doomed to live in a fallen world, but by knowing he *is* a fallen man in a fallen world. . . ."[4]

Third, if grace is amazing, we should ask God to penetrate that truth so deeply into our souls that it drives out other emotions that could pollute our evangelistic efforts.

---

[4] C. S. Lewis, *The World's Last Night and Other Essays* (New York: Harcourt Brace Jovanovich, 1960), 77.

In particular, grace should serve as the antidote to fear and guilt, two common obstacles to fruitful witness.

Many people told me they didn't witness to their family simply because they were afraid to. When I probed a bit, I did not find their families to be particularly evil or sinister. Instead, a vague cloud of fear loomed that immobilized the Christian from ever saying anything about the Lord. That cloud lifted when it was identified as an idol—the idol of fear of what relatives would think.

If this sounds accurate, don't try to muster up courage. That's what many people try—with little or no success. Instead, soak in grace. Remind yourself that your standing before God was provided by the finished work of the cross. You didn't earn or manufacture salvation. The atonement paid for all your sins, including the idolatry of other people's opinions of you.

Try to visualize a list of your sins nailed to the cross (see Col. 2:14). See "the fear of other peoples' disapproval" on that list. Ask God to move you from fears to tears—tears of compassion for your family who would benefit from the same liberation God has brought to you.

Apply this same gospel-grace to all the guilt you feel for not witnessing more or better or consistently or brilliantly or whatever else starts the flow of bottomless guilt. As I talked to people who actually had seen family members come to faith, I marveled at how guilty they still felt.

Ali told me of how he saw his Muslim mother come to faith at age eighty-eight, and yet he still felt guilty about all his other relatives who rejected his witnessing overtures. As the pastor of a small congregation of former Muslims, Ali has seen remarkable numbers of conversions among the Muslim community of a large East Coast city. Having come to faith during college, Ali eventually transferred to Bible college and then went into ministry in a highly resistant mission field. His brothers mocked him and his father disowned him, but his mother listened—for over four decades before accepting "Esa" (Jesus) as her Savior.

Ali recounted the sermons he preached at his father's and mother's funerals, the way his congregation reached out in love to his Muslim relatives, and how several of them marveled at how accepting and loving and generous these people were—even though they were reaching out to people who thought of them as infidels.

Still, when I asked Ali what advice he would give to others who wanted to witness to Muslim relatives, he shrugged his shoulders and mumbled, "I don't know. My efforts have been so lame. I should have done so much more."

This kind of guilt is not from God. It is not the "godly grief" that "produces repentance" (2 Cor. 7:10). Instead, this form of guilt comes from the "accuser of our brothers" (Rev. 12:10) and should be countered with the pronouncements of "no condemnation" (Rom. 8:1) that flow from the gospel. Such guilt may also flow from the kind of pride that causes us to think that *we* are the prime mover for salvation for our relatives. Jesus died for that idolatry as well.

The gospel can move us from guilt to tears just as it moves us from fears to tears. But these tears are sad ones rather than guilty ones. Sadness is a far more healthy and productive emotion than guilt or fear. Sadness is right and appropriate when we think of loved ones separated from the Lord. It drives us to our knees in prayer for the lost and loosens our lips to say words of grace. Ask God to replace your fear and guilt with sadness and compassion. Grace can help make that divine exchange.

Perhaps the following story can help you sense both the amazing and breaking dimensions of grace.

One cold February night, not all that long ago, our youngest son, Jon, called home just before midnight and sent an earthquake through our family with these words: "Dad. I need you to come pick me up. The police caught me smoking weed." I had fallen asleep on our living room couch, but now I was wide awake. "Who is this?" I stammered, hoping someone had called a wrong number. Surely, this must be some other person's son. "It's Jon, Dad," he replied. "I'm so sorry."

That began a lengthy and painful family upheaval, complete with consultations with lawyers, therapists, law enforcement officials, and ultimately, a long trip to "escort" our son to one of those boarding schools for troubled teens.

We had no clue that Jon had developed a drug habit that had engulfed his life. In a short amount of time, he had progressed from merely dabbling with marijuana to smoking every day—five, six, or more times each day not only to "get high" but to maintain a level of dependence on the drug. (Yes. Contrary to the ever-increasing propaganda, you can become dependent on marijuana and it can damage the brain terribly, especially at the crucial stage of development of adolescence. It's amazing how much I ended up learning about the drug and that entire culture over the next several months.)[5]

The school Jon attended was part of a network of programs that sought to help entire families, not just the troubled teen. Pam and I attended numerous parenting workshops offered to help us rebuild our relationship with our son. We found, in those gatherings, a level of support and honesty that has marked us in very good ways ever since.

At the first gathering of over two hundred parents, I found myself filled with judgmental thoughts. "These people are terrible," I muttered. "They must be horrible parents. All their kids are drug addicts!"

---

[5] Although this is far from the topic of this book, I can't pass up the opportunity to recommend a book that was very helpful for me: Timmen L. Cermak, *Marijuana: What's a Parent to Believe?* (Center City, MN: Hazelden, 2003). It is part of the Informed Parent series of books. Although I have not read any others in the series, my guess would be that they are all a blend of accurate scientific information and compassionate insight for parents. John Vawter's excellent ministry, You're Not Alone, was also invaluable to us during those difficult days (see www.notalone.org).

During one of the breaks, we compared stories with a single mom whose son had just tried to quit his gang. She feared for his life, since other gang members who quit were promptly murdered. As this woman nervously took drags on her cigarette, I noticed a ring with a pentagram on it (a symbol of satanic worship), which complimented her orange-dyed hair, crystal earrings, and black lipstick. She had told us, earlier during the seminar, that she was indeed a witch and found her religion to be very helpful for handling the stress of having a son involved in drugs and gangs.

I listened to her story while hearing two very clear statements crisscross in my mind. The first one sarcastically announced, "Well, no wonder your son is so screwed up, lady. What do you expect? You're a satanic witch!" The second statement was softer but no less clear: "So, Randy, what are you doing here?"

It was a painful moment. I replayed the previous judgmental statements that had been resounding in my head throughout the seminar. I was embarrassed and wanted to run away.

This seminar did indeed allow you to run away—but only to process your inner reflections about the day's proceedings. Each evening, we had to go back to our rooms and write a prescribed number of pages in a journal, evaluating what we had experienced and learned that day. I processed my encounter with the witch by beginning my journal entry with these words:

"Randy, you self-righteous jackass!"

I continued by trying to make sense of the woman's choice of religions. Here's what I wrote in my journal:

"What is it about witchcraft that could be so appealing to an intelligent, rational woman? Well . . . actually it makes sense when I give it some thought. Witchcraft offers a kind of power, a sense of control. It helps people feel secure in a chaotic world. It also must have a certain kind of appeal because it makes you feel better than other people. It makes you feel superior. Am I condoning this? No. I'm not saying that this is good. I'm just saying that it makes sense. I don't think it's good at all. It's very bad. In fact it's so bad, I think this woman needs the gospel. Her witchcraft is idolatry. It's worshiping herself instead of God. It's sin. In fact, it's so bad that nothing short of the death of the Son of God could possibly pay for her sin."

I felt rather wise at that point. But I still had several pages of written processing to do in order to fulfill the requirement of the assignment. I continued:

"What is it about my judgmentalism that could be so appealing to an intelligent, rational Christian man like me? Well . . . actually it makes sense when I give it some thought. Judgmentalism offers a kind of power, a sense of control. It helps people feel secure in a chaotic world. It also must have a certain kind of appeal because it makes you feel better than other people. It makes you feel superior. Am I condoning this? No. I'm not saying that this is good. I'm just saying that it makes sense. I don't think it's good at all. It's very bad. In fact it's so bad, I think I need the gospel. My judgmentalism is idolatry. It's worshiping myself instead of God. It's sin. In fact, it's so bad that nothing short of the death of the Son of God could possibly pay for my sin."

I dropped my pen on my journal. Something transformative began to happen when I saw that my sin needed the same solution as hers. I kept saying, "My sin is so bad, it needs a cross . . . and that's exactly what I have."

The next day I sat next to the witch during the morning session. I was honestly glad to see her. I asked her if the seminar was helpful to her. She said it was. I told her it was helpful for me as well. We talked about our sons—how concerned we were for them, how well they were now doing, and how we couldn't wait to see them again. I have thought of her and her son and prayed for them many times since then.

Grace, at that seminar, amazed me and broke me. I hope I never forget it.

So, what did I tell the anesthesiologist after he injected me? How did I respond after he asked me if I thought people who danced, drank, or smoked would go to hell?

I said this:

"Well, I think we all like rules because they make it easy to know who's in and who's out. We like rules because they can make us feel superior to those people who don't keep them. In fact, I think I make all sorts of rules that I generally keep because they make me feel good about me and bad about others." I could see I had grabbed his attention.

"But the stuff I need forgiveness for is a whole lot worse than just smoking or dancing or drinking. I need to be forgiven for anger, bitterness, hatred, self-righteousness. . . ." I stopped. His face looked shocked.

"No. Really." I continued. "If I'm going to have any kind of connection with God, I need forgiveness for some really ugly attitudes and actions. That's why I really like Christianity. It offers that kind of forgiveness."

Dr. Leonard thanked me and told me I had given him something to think about. I continue to pray for him as well.

Isn't grace amazing—and breaking? Isn't it absolutely breathtaking that a holy righteous God forgives people like me . . . and you! Doesn't that just break your pride and arrogance and self-absorption! Doesn't that kind of news sound really good? Doesn't it change your tone of voice and posture as you tell your family that Jesus died for them? Until the grace of God strikes you as both amazing and breaking, it may be best for you to just pray for your family. Pray that God brings others into their lives to witness to them while he works in your life to fill you with wonder and joy.

Steps to Take

1. Pray that the "eyes of your heart [will be] enlightened, that you may know what is the hope to which he has called you . . ." (see Eph.1:18–19). Ask God to overwhelm you with all that you have in Christ so that it starts to change your tone of voice and choice of vocabulary in conversations with your family.

2. Pray for God to bring other grace-amazed Christians into the lives of your family members.

3. Memorize a concise statement of the gospel you can repeat to yourself. One I frequently meditate upon is, "My sin is so bad that nothing short of the death of the son of God could pay for it, and that's exactly what I have."

4. Understate. Try some shorter, incomplete, statements that point your family toward the gospel. Especially at the early stages of your interaction with your family, "less is more."

5. Experiment. Try to point out some evidences of common grace (a beautiful scene, a delicious meal, a moving novel [other than a Christian one!]), and see how they respond to your "telling it slant."

TRUTH

Liberating and Yet Narrow

The words, "Thou shalt not talk" appear nowhere in the Washington, DC, subway system. But that unwritten command hangs in the air and, consequently, hardly anyone ever talks while riding the Metro. Daily commuters read *The Washington Post* or the latest political thriller or an official classified document, but talking is seldom heard.

So I, along with all the other Metro riders, responded with fear and trepidation one morning when a man stepped onto the subway car and announced, "May I have your attention please!" Even if the security rating hadn't just been elevated to the orange level, anyone would have been frightened. But the woman sitting next to me responded in a way I'll never forget. She started screaming (and that is no exaggeration), "No! Stop! Don't!"

Everyone darted their eyes between the screaming woman and the attention-seeking man. He reached into his pocket. (Never had the assurance of my salvation seemed so precious to me!) He pulled out a book. (I fully expected to see a bomb.)

And he began to sing, "Blessed assurance, Jesus is mine. Oh, what a foretaste of glory divine."

Everyone breathed a sigh of relief. Everyone except the woman sitting next to me. She continued to scream for the man to stop. It was the oddest duet I have ever heard.

"Heir of salvation, purchase of God. . . ."

"Shut up. Stop."

"Born of his spirit, washed in his blood."

"Somebody put a sock in his mouth!"

As our rush-hour evangelist came to the end of the fourth stanza (even Fanny Crosby, the hymn's composer, would have been impressed), our train arrived at the next stop. As the Metro car doors opened and the man stepped out of the car, he announced to everyone, "Have a blessed day." His duet partner, sitting next to me, calmed down and announced, "I have to put up with that stuff every day." (Although, I believe her vocabulary choice was something other than "stuff.")

As I looked around the subway car, I was quite certain that almost everyone identified more with the screaming woman than the melodious evangelist. Her loud ranting disturbed them far less than his pious singing.

We could probably debate the pros and cons of this method of mass-transit evangelism, but I'll leave that for others. My point in telling this story is to highlight the response. At least one person thought this pronouncement of good news was anything but good. And I suspect she's not alone in her disdain for evangelism. In most settings, we've moved from "live and let live" to "Keep it to yourself, Buddy!"

That is certainly the case within many families. Home may be where bonds are closest, but it's also where fuses are shortest. How do we proclaim truth in a hostile environment, even if that environment is filled with the smell of apple pie?

It's not just hostility toward evangelism that people feel. At least two other factors make evangelism an uphill battle— exclusivity and truth-fatigue. In this age of pluralism, exclusivity remains the only cardinal sin you must not commit. Truth-fatigue plagues us because we just don't believe *anyone* anymore—about anything! We don't believe baseball players when they tell us they don't use steroids. We don't believe politicians when they tell us they've been faithful to their spouses. We don't believe movie stars when they tell us their marriage "has never been better." It's only a matter of time before they all appear before cameras and tell us "mistakes were made."

Into this atmosphere of intolerance, relativism, and skepticism, Christians dare to believe and proclaim that Jesus is the way, the truth, and the life. Some reflection on the nature of gospel-truth may arm us for the difficult task of evangelism in the twenty-first century. We can learn a great deal from the way the apostle Paul proclaimed gospel-truth in Athens. His audience and your family may have a great deal in common.

Luke's account in Acts 17 begins with a report of what was going on inside the apostle. He was disturbed by all the idols he saw in Athens. Don't let this observation fly by without some reflection. We, too, need to see idolatry for what it is—not just in the lives of others but in our own hearts as well. Only then can we proclaim our message with sympathy instead of superiority.

Then Luke gives us an account of the words Paul spoke:[1]

Men of Athens, I perceive that in every way you are very religious. For as I passed along and observed the objects of your worship, I found also an altar with this inscription, "To the unknown god." What therefore you worship as unknown, this I proclaim to you. The God who made the world and everything in it, being Lord of heaven and earth, does not live in temples made by man, nor is

---

[1] I will not attempt a thorough exposition of this important passage. My aim is to identify just a few highlights. For a fuller treatment, see D. A. Carson, "Athens Revisited" in *Telling the Truth*, ed. D. A. Carson (Grand Rapids, MI: Zondervan, 2002); John R. W. Stott, *The Message of Acts: The Spirit, the Church, and the World* (Downers Grove, IL: InterVarsity Press, 1990); and Ajith Fernando, *Acts*, The NIV Application Commentary (Grand Rapids, MI: Zondervan, 1998).

he served by human hands, as though he needed anything, since he himself gives to all mankind life and breath and everything. And he made from one man every nation of mankind to live on all the face of the earth, having determined allotted periods and the boundaries of their dwelling place, that they should seek God, in the hope that they might feel their way toward him and find him. Yet he is actually not far from each one of us, for

"In him we live and move and have our being";

as even some of your own poets have said,

"For we are indeed his offspring."

Being then God's offspring, we ought not to think that the divine being is like gold or silver or stone, an image formed by the art and imagination of man. The times of ignorance God overlooked, but now he commands all people everywhere to repent, because he has fixed a day on which he will judge the world in righteousness by a man whom he has appointed; and of this he has given assurance to all by raising him from the dead. (Acts 17:22–31)

From this text, I draw at least five pertinent conclusions.

Gospel-Truth Has Substance

In many ways, our world today is more like Athens than Jerusalem. When Paul preached in Jewish settings, he quoted Scripture and employed biblical lines of reasoning. His subtext was, "This message about Jesus flows from the very Scriptures you already know and love."

But in Athens, Paul looked elsewhere for common ground. He quoted their poets, observed their statues, and used their method of reasoning. Ajith Fernando comments, "When Paul evangelized this city of Socrates he used the method of Socrates."[2]

Paul also blazed a new path, one that contradicted their assumptions. The Athenians "would spend their time in noth-

---

[2] Fernando, *Acts*, 474.

ing except telling or hearing something new" (Acts 17:21). In other words, they enjoyed the search but doubted whether anything could be found. Paul told them his message had substance and the search could find something. This sounded as countercultural in Athens back then as it might in your living room today.

Paul began by claiming we *can* know some things: "What therefore you worship as unknown, this I proclaim to you" (v. 23). Most commentators believe Luke recorded only a summary of a much longer speech. If you read what Luke wrote in Acts 17, it only takes about three minutes. But knowing what we do about Mars Hill in Paul's day, it is more likely that he spoke for ten times that amount. I would imagine that Paul massaged this point a bit before moving on. In a sense, he had to get them to grant him the possibility that substantive truth exists.

We may need to do the same thing *before* we get to the heart of our message. (See chap. 6 for a fuller treatment of ways to "put in the clutch before shifting gears.") Sometimes asking a few questions can open the door for more receptive hearts and minds. Here are a few that may be worth trying out:

"I agree that seeking truth is important. Do you think it's possible to ever find truth?"

"You talk a lot about seeking. Do you also expect to find?"

"Wouldn't it make sense that, if there is a God, he would make it possible for us to find him?"

Only after Paul suggests that the Athenians don't need to worship an unknown God does he offer the substance-laden alternative. He proclaims a worldview that moves from creation to resurrection. He does not assume they already know and believe what the Scriptures say about God. He begins with a basic primer on theology, moves on to offer insight about human nature, and then talks about Jesus. We would do well to emulate his sequence and flow of thought.

We must proclaim the gospel differently today than we did just a few decades ago. It used to be that we could assume people knew the content of the biblical message and we merely needed to defend it. Today we dare not skip to defending if we have not first declared. This is what Paul did in Athens.

It's as if he said, "Let me tell you what kind of God I'm talking about." Or, "Many people mean many different things when they use the word 'god.' Let me tell you what I mean when I use that word." He lists several truths he holds about God—all of which differed from the Athenians' Epicurean and Stoic views.

The God Paul proclaimed:

- Is knowable (see vv. 23, 27).
- Created everything (see v. 24).
- Rules over everything he made (see vv. 24–25).
- Created us (see v. 25).
- Doesn't need us (see v. 25).
- Is our ultimate source of life, sustenance, meaning, and purpose (see vv. 27–28).
- Determines times and places that people will live (see v. 26).
- Is not like idols of gold, silver, or stone (see v. 29).

Can you see why this view of God threatened ancient philosophers and could do the same to your relatives? But wait. It gets worse.

This God also:

- Commands all people to repent (see v. 30).
- Will judge the world (see v. 31).
- Confirmed the coming judgment with Jesus' resurrection (see v. 31).

C. S. Lewis grasped the discomfort this truth causes when he wrote, "An 'impersonal God'—well and good. A subjective

God of beauty, truth and goodness, inside our own heads—better still. A formless life-force surging through us, a vast power which we can tap—best of all. But God Himself, alive, pulling at the other end of the cord, perhaps approaching at an infinite speed, the hunter, king, husband—that's quite another matter."[3]

John Stott, commenting on Paul's Mars Hill sermon, sums up our need to proclaim a substantive gospel with this theological insight: "Now all this is part of the gospel. Or at least it is the indispensable background to the gospel, without which the gospel cannot effectively be preached. Many people are rejecting our gospel today not because they perceive it to be false, but because they perceive it to be trivial. People are looking for an integrated worldview, which makes sense of all their experience. We learn from Paul that we cannot preach the gospel of Jesus without the doctrine of God, or the cross without the creation, or salvation without judgment. Today's world needs a bigger gospel, the full gospel of Scripture, what Paul later in Ephesus was to call 'the whole purpose of God' (20:27, NEB)."[4]

Gospel-Truth Draws Lines

I have already mentioned that Paul's truth differed from his audience's. That's why some of them "mocked" when he spoke of the resurrection. The gospel always divides. And this will always be uncomfortable—for both the evangelist and the listener. While it helps to find common ground, a point will come where our path and our non-Christian relatives' paths diverge. This is nothing new. People have always bristled at our exclusive gospel. That's why they tried to throw Jesus off a cliff (Luke 4:29). It's why they stoned Stephen (Acts 7:58). It's why they tried to kill Paul several times (e.g. Acts

---

[3] C. S. Lewis, *Miracles* (San Francisco: HarperCollins, 2001), 94.
[4] Stott, *Message of Acts*, 290.

14:19, 21:31). And it may explain why tension fills your family gatherings.

I say all this because we need to recognize and resist the temptation to compromise evangelistically. We all feel the tug to back off and just stay with the comfortable parts of our message. ("God loves you. I love you. Let's just laugh and enjoy one another.")

Michael told me how sad he always feels whenever he witnesses to his sister Louise. They have such a good relationship otherwise. They laugh a lot together and have many common interests—favorite movies, music groups, songs, etc. Michael has found many ways to weave the gospel into their conversations and Louise is always very interested. She's sincerely curious but never compelled to believe. And Michael always walks away with an ache inside. This is probably unavoidable but should never be debilitating. If the sadness of another's lost condition tempts you to compromise, perhaps you've made comfort into an idol. Comfort and evangelism seldom go together.

The temptation to compromise also has a theological component. You'll wonder if your saintly uncle might find God through some other means or religion. It's even more tempting if he happens to be a fairly upright, moral guy or a devout observer of another faith. But attempts to compromise the exclusive claims of Jesus and the New Testament writers fail to overturn the age-old position of the church. There is indeed "salvation in no one else, for there is no other name under heaven given among men by which we must be saved" (Acts 4:12).[5]

---

[5] This issue is worthy of thorough investigation—especially if you're longing for theologically deep answers to difficult questions. For a fuller treatment see Robertson McQuilken, "The Narrow Way" in *Perspectives on the World Christian Movement: A Reader* (Pasadena, CA: William Carey Library, 2009), 156–61; and Harold A. Netland, "One Lord and Savior for All? Jesus Christ and Religious Diversity," The Gospel Coalition, December 17, 2009, http://thegospelcoalition.org/resources/a/httpthegospelcoalition .orgpublicationsccione_lord_and_savior_for_all/.

Two clarifying questions may help us wrestle with the exclusivity of the gospel: Must the resurrection inevitably lead to exclusivity? And must pluralism inevitably lead to relativism? The answer to the first question is yes. The answer to the second one is no. Allow me to explain.

We note that Paul's audience responded after he spoke of the resurrection. (Some mocked, some wanted more info, some believed). Why is that? Because Jesus' resurrection separates him from all other religious figures and it distinguishes his method of salvation from all others'. Only Jesus conquered death, so only in Jesus can we overcome that inevitable fate. His resurrection validated the atoning nature of his death. It wasn't just some political martyrdom. It satisfied a holy God's wrath. Without the resurrection, the cross seems pointless or merely something that evokes pity rather than trust.

The resurrection also shows the impotence of a works-based righteousness. As Paul reasoned, "if righteousness were through the law, then Christ died for no purpose" (Gal. 2:21). In other words, if there were some way for your upright moral uncle to make it to heaven as a man of integrity or a devout churchgoer (or Buddhist or Muslim or Jew, etc.), then Jesus' death would turn out to be unnecessary.

If you don't already have some concise things to say about the resurrection, you should do some homework and make that part of your apologetics tool bag. It will help transfer your evangelistic conversations away from vague philosophy to the more concrete realm of history.[6]

We need a kind of reasoning to make sense of Jesus' exclusive claim: "No one comes to the Father except through me" (John 14:6). Many Christians are reluctant to do so. The eminent sociologist Robert Withnow observed, "When asked why they think it is necessary to believe in Jesus to be saved, the most typical response of Christians with an exclusivist worldview is to refer to the Bible, not to elaborate

---

[6] See William Lane Craig, *A Reasonable Faith* (Wheaton, IL: Crossway, 2008), 333.

or try to explain why the Bible says what it does, but simply to assert that the Bible is their source as if saying anything more would somehow diminish the flat fact of the Bible's absolute veracity."[7]

But Jesus himself, in the very same context of John 14, appealed to logic and reason to back up his claim. Paul used an extended argument in Romans 1–4 to show how reason leads to the conclusion that there is only one way to heaven. We need to find ways to articulate the internally consistent logic of the gospel's claims and not resort to anti-intellectual punch lines like, "The Bible says it, I believe it, and that settles it."

Here are a few ways we might ease into this exclusive message without sounding angry or dogmatic:

"I know what I'm saying sounds narrow, but have you ever wondered *why* Jesus claimed to be the only way to God?" (This puts the weight of the argument on Jesus instead of you.)

"Yes. This does sound exclusive. But there are many areas of life where exclusive answers are what we really need. I want exclusive doctors who only prescribe the medicines that will cure me. Don't you?"

"Well, let's just suspend this argument for a little bit and let me tell you why this makes sense to me. See if you can give me the benefit of the doubt for five minutes."

The second question, whether pluralism inevitably leads to relativism, requires more attention than it did a few decades ago. With changes in immigration legislation, increased ease of travel, and the globalizing effects of the Internet, our world has evolved into a multicultural mix that demands careful thought about different religions. It was one thing to think that Hindus, Buddhists, Muslims, and others were "lost" when

---

[7] Robert Wuthnow, *America and the Challenges of Religious Diversity* (Princeton, NJ: Princeton University Press, 2007), 177.

they lived thousands of miles away. But now that they live next door, post blogs in our language, and build centers of worship down the street, we need to think deeply about this "only one way" stuff.

Most people today state rather assuredly that all ways lead to God. But the assumption behind this claim needs to be challenged. We need to be wary of a kind of chronological snobbery, which looks down its nose on people in the past. Your sister-in-law might say, "Yes. I know Christians used to be so imperialistic as to think theirs was the only correct path. But now we've evolved past that kind of arrogance." We should respond by pointing out the arrogance in her statement. Again, questions might help here:

"But Sarah, aren't you being just as arrogant to say that Christians are wrong for saying others are wrong?"

"But Dad, how can you say that? Your view that all religions are equal is actually quite new and rare. Most religious people for the vast majority of history have believed theirs was the only way. Your post-Enlightenment American view is really the intolerant one."

"Cousin Susan, listen. You keep saying how open-minded your Buddhist friends are. Have you ever read what the Dalai Lama says about other religions? He thinks they're all wrong. Only Buddhism saves!"[8]

This is difficult to get across. Your family, like mine, has been so steeped in the era of "tolerance" they will resist your line of logic with emotional intensity. Still, it is necessary work in these pluralistic days. Some people need to see their own

---

[8] When asked about other religions' ability to provide refuge, the Dalai Lama replied, "Liberation in which 'a mind that understands the sphere of reality annihilates all defilements in the sphere of reality' is a state that only Buddhists can accomplish. This kind of *moksha* or *nirvana* is only explained in the Buddhist scriptures, and is achieved only through Buddhist practice," His Holiness the XIVth Dalai Lama, "'Religious Harmony' and Extracts from *The Bodhgaya Interviews*," in *Christianity through Non-Christian Eyes*, ed. Paul J. Griffiths (Maryknoll, NY: Orbis Books, 1990), 169. Quoted in Keith Yandell and Harold Netland, *Buddhism: A Christian Exploration and Appraisal* (Downers Grove, IL: InterVarsity Press, 2009), 109.

pride below the surface of their "open-mindedness" before they'll see their own need for the Savior.

Marty's brother Ken returned from a postcollege tour of Israel and renounced his evangelical faith because of all the many religions he saw practiced there. All those Orthodox Jews and devout Muslims couldn't all be wrong, he concluded, and changed his plans from enrolling in seminary to applying to grad school to study anthropology. Marty and Ken's dialogue sounded something like this:

Ken: All our lives we've been told we need to evangelize people of other religions, but you didn't see what I saw in Jerusalem.

Marty: What did you see?

Ken: All those Jews crying out to God at the Wailing Wall and all those Muslims praying at the Al-Aqsa Mosque. You just can't tell me they're all lost.

Marty: Why not? Are you saying that everyone who prays believes the truth?

Ken: You didn't see how sincere they were.

Marty: How could you tell what was going on in their hearts? By how loud they were praying?

Ken: Have you ever been to Jerusalem?

Marty: No. But plenty of Christians have been to Jerusalem and saw the same things you saw and they didn't draw the same conclusion. In fact, Christians who *live* in Jerusalem, the ones who actually know those people, reach out and evangelize their Jewish and Muslim neighbors and friends quite a lot.

Ken: Look. I used to believe all that Great Commission stuff. But now that I've seen those people face to face, I just can't anymore.

Marty: Are you saying you're more enlightened than the Scriptures? They make it rather clear that we should bring the gospel to the Middle East.

Ken: Hmm.

Marty: Is it possible you're elevating your experience over Jesus' authority?

Ken: That's a pretty serious charge.

Marty: I know. But it's worth considering, isn't it? You're not the first person to go to Jerusalem or Mecca or Beijing or anywhere else and wonder about people of other religions.

Ken: Maybe. But it's all so overwhelming.

Marty: I'll agree with you there. But that's not a good enough reason to reject what Jesus and Paul said and what the vast majority of Christians have believed ever since.

Maybe you can't confront your relatives as bluntly as Marty did. A lot depends on your family dynamics, cultural norms, and your specific relationship with the relative you're addressing. But the notion that pluralism *must* lead to relativism needs to be refuted. Otherwise your exclusive gospel will remain, in the minds of your relatives, a form of bigotry, intolerance, and narrow-mindedness they won't even consider.

Gospel-Truth Illumines Everything

If John Stott's assertion that people are looking for an "integrated worldview, which makes sense of all their experience" is true, we should show how the gospel illumines all areas of life. Our message promises far more than just a ticket to heaven.

Many people have seen the biblical worldview as a four-stage drama, moving from creation to fall to redemption to consummation. But often, Christians present a truncated gospel that only includes the second and third components. So, our gospel sounds as simplistic as, "You've sinned. Jesus died for your sins. Pray this prayer and you won't go to hell for your sins." To some extent, all that is true. But in many ears, it rings shallow or, as Stott says, "trivial." People reject it because it doesn't connect to the many facets of their lives.

This is not mere pragmatism. Theological connections between others' life experiences and the gospel already exist, and we need to highlight them. The areas of their lives we often pass over connect profoundly to the creation and consummation parts of our message.

Non-Christians long to make sense of their lives and wonder where they fit into this big, beautiful, awe-inspiring world. That's because they were created by a personal God who placed them into a created world with his fingerprints all over it. They also long for relief from suffering and the realization of ultimate justice. That's because this world is headed toward a consummation, and God has placed eternity in their hearts (see Eccles. 3:11).

That's why Paul quoted Athenian poets—not just because they were *their* poets and easily recognizable. That is certainly true. Much more could be said about our need to quote today's poets (or, better yet, the song writers and movie makers) and show how they point us to the gospel. But notice which particular truths Paul chose to quote: "In him we live and move and have our being" and "For we are indeed his offspring" (Acts 17:28).

Paul showed how the gospel relates to a wider range of topics than just getting into heaven—everything that fits under "live, move, and have our being." The gospel relates to and satisfies our wonderings about why we are here, how we make sense of life, and where we are going. Especially with relatives who may have already heard our rants about heaven and hell, we could gain greater traction speaking about a host of other topics from a gospel-based worldview. Call it "going in the side door" or "doing an end run" or whatever you wish, showing how the gospel makes sense of all areas of their lives may succeed where other frontal assaults have failed.

For years, even decades, Ralph tried to preach the gospel to his brother Ed. Nothing got through. In fact, Ed made it perfectly clear he wasn't interested. Then one day, on a long car ride together, Ralph sensed a different way to proceed. (By the way, many people told me their best conversations occurred in a car—where both people faced forward, rather than toward each other. Perhaps the indirect eye contact posed less of a threat.)

Ed had just told Ralph of struggles in his marriage. He and his wife had actually separated for a while and wondered if they could ever get back together. Ralph shocked his brother by telling him of the difficulties in his marriage as well. Ed thought his brother and sister-in-law never had such struggles, and, in fact, the appearance of a perfect marriage had made Ed less likely to broach this subject.

Ralph told his brother something like this: "You know, when our marriage is good, there's nothing better in the whole world. It's as if we were made for each other and made for the kind of intimacy that marriage provides. But when we're at odds with each other, it's the most painful thing in the world. We treat each other worse than we would treat our enemies. I think the only thing that has kept us together all these years is that we've learned some things about how to forgive each other."

After some discussion, he added: "I think our faith really helps us a lot here. Knowing how God forgives us helps us forgive each other. Without that, we would have split a long time ago."

Ralph told me his vulnerability about his sinfulness and his appreciation for God's forgiveness enabled him to present more of the gospel to his brother than any direct approach he'd tried before. He also added, "It helped that I didn't condemn him for separating from his wife. Instead, I identified with his struggle to make marriage work. I share the same struggles. I just have a resource he hasn't found yet."

Showing how a comprehensive gospel illumines all areas of life may be the key that opens a door for relatives who have previously rejected our message.

Nelson certainly found that to be true. His nephew Drew admired him because of his keen intellect and role as a professor at a major university. Drew would ask his uncle questions about academic issues and current events because he respected his thoughtful insights. He even came to him for advice about dating.

"I can't seem to settle down with just one woman," he told him with a hint of desperation. "I date a woman for six months and then lose interest in her. At first it's a challenge and then it's a conquest. But once that happens, I start looking elsewhere."

Now that Drew was in his early thirties and wanting to settle down, he found his pattern of dating a source of deep discouragement.

"It sounds like you're telling me that you sleep with these women," Nelson pointedly observed.

After the shock wore off, Drew acknowledged that yes, indeed, he did have sex with the women he dated.

"Why don't you try *not* having sex with a woman and see how that works out," Nelson suggested. That sparked a rather lengthy discussion about the nature of sex and how it can have two opposite effects in relationships. In lifelong commitments of marriage, Nelson explained, sex serves as a kind of glue that bonds a man and a woman together in mysterious ways. It promotes intimacy and trust. For single people who have not made such a commitment, sex does just the opposite. It compartmentalizes, fragments, and drives a wedge between people instead of uniting them.

Nelson freely told his nephew that choosing to wait until he found a woman with whom he could share every area of his life (not just his bed) before having sex could be the alternative approach he's been looking for.

As hard as it may be to imagine someone like Drew choosing abstinence until marriage, that's exactly what he did. And, just like Uncle Nelson said, a relationship of trust and intimacy emerged. He found a woman he could really get to know and enjoy totally outside of his bedroom. And he married her. Then, he started asking his uncle where he got such crazy ideas. The way Drew describes the process, their conversations went from dating and sex to the Bible and the gospel. He reasoned that, if the Bible and his uncle could be right about something like sex, they might also be right about God. The first book of the Bible Drew read was the Song of Solomon. The second one was the Gospel of John. It was after reading that second book that Drew became a Christian.

We need to demonstrate how the gospel relates to all areas of life. This takes some prior reflection—but it would be mental energy that will prompt wonder and worship on your part and insight that could lead to salvation for your loved ones. For, if indeed God is the "one who made the world and *everything* in it" (Acts 17:24), then *everything* can point us to him and his salvation. No wonder C. S. Lewis said, "I believe in Christianity as I believe that the Sun has risen, not only because I see it, but because by it I see everything else."[9]

Gospel-Truth Prompts a Response

Some of Paul's Athenian listeners mocked. Some wanted to hear more. And some believed. Gospel-truth always works that way. Because it begins with a prognosis of the worst kind ("you're sinful and in need of total regeneration") and progresses to a solution based on a cross ("there's nothing you can do to save yourself"), gospel-truth tends to polarize

---

[9] C. S. Lewis, *The Weight of Glory and Other Essays* (New York: HarperCollins, 1949), 140.

people. We need to anticipate this, because it can feel painful to have close relatives respond so strongly.

If our brother or mother or anyone else hears our message as good news, we rejoice. We tell them to express saving faith through a short prayer like one found in the back of a gospel tract. We guide them to trust in what Christ did on the cross. If our family members have been trusting in other things to satisfy their longings, gospel-truth slakes the thirst that comes from trying to drink from "cisterns that can hold no water" (see Jer. 2:13).

But we must also realize that gospel-truth, by its very essence, has the potential to harden. This is so counterintuitive to most Christians' ways of thinking that it demands special consideration.

When Jesus made seemingly audacious claims about himself before a religious audience, they took refuge in their Abrahamic heritage. By saying, "Abraham is our father" (John 8:39), they claimed a right standing with God already. They rejected the notion of any need for Jesus, even though he had just announced that "everyone who commits sin is a slave to sin" but "if the Son sets you free, you will be free indeed" (John 8:34, 36).

As Jesus turned up the heat, delineating the sharp contrast between being "his disciples" (John 8:31) and being "of your father the devil" (v. 44), he dared to say, "But *because* I tell you the truth, you do not believe me" (v. 45). He did not say, "although I tell you the truth" but "*because* I tell you the truth."

Commentator D. A. Carson explains, "The children of God will so love the truth that they will believe in Jesus; the children of the Devil will be so characterized by lies that they will not be able to accept the truth, precisely *because it is the truth.*"[10]

---

[10] D. A. Carson, *The Gospel according to John* (Grand Rapids, MI.: Eerdmans, 1991), 353–54. Emphasis his.

For some people, gospel-truth demands too great a sacrifice. They must let go of the sin they have grown to love. For some, it requires too great a change. They have trod so long and so stubbornly along a certain path, that to change now seems impossible or humiliating. And for some, gospel-truth just seems too good to be true. The darkness of sin and its consequences have made some people so jaded, they can't open themselves to potential disappointment. If the gospel you're telling them were to let them down after they give it a try, it would be too crushing a blow. They'd rather wallow in the familiar mess they're in than to venture to an unknown way of life—no matter how good you tell them it is.

In the character of Kate in his disturbing novel *East of Eden*, John Steinbeck painted a torturesome portrait of this kind of rejection of goodness. After just a short time of being married to her husband Adam, she slept with his brother Charles and became pregnant with twin sons. Adam never suspected they were not his offspring. She left him, after attempting to kill him, and took up a life of prostitution. Eventually sinking to the role of a madam in a whorehouse, her life became engulfed in crime, blackmail, drug addiction, and even murder.

When Charles, her brother-in-law and the father of her children died, he left his brother and Kate a sizable amount of money, not knowing of their separation or her despicable life. Technically, Adam could have kept all the money for himself but chose instead to deliver Kate's portion to her.

As he did, Kate scoffed at him and wondered what his real motives were:

> "I want you to have what is yours. Charles willed you the money. It isn't mine."
>
> "I'll find the trick. I'll find it."
>
> "I guess you can't understand it. I don't much care. There are so many things I don't understand. I don't understand how you could shoot me and desert your sons. I don't understand

how you or anyone could live like this." He waved his hand to indicate the house. . . .

After a bit more of interchange between them, most of which was Kate's venomous verbal abuse, Adam said,

> "I said I didn't understand about you," he said slowly. "Just now it came to me what you don't understand. . . . You know about the ugliness in people . . . but you—yes, that's right—you don't know about the rest. You don't believe I brought you the letter because I don't want your money. You don't believe I loved you. And the men who come to you here with their ugliness . . . you don't believe those men could have goodness and beauty in them. You see only one side, and you think—more than that, you're sure—that's all there is."[11]

Few people can rival Kate for her depth of resentment. But gospel-truth can harden some people just as dramatically as it can heal others. Don't let this truth discourage you. It should motivate you to pray more fervently while proclaiming more gently. It should also forearm you to handle extreme responses with grace and love.

Gospel-Truth Is Easy to Miss

Soon after my wife and I moved to the Washington, DC, area, we went downtown to a play at the Kennedy Center. We drove eastbound on route 66, went over the Theodore Roosevelt bridge, and saw the beautiful building overlooking the Potomac River.

"There it is!" I exclaimed, partly out of appreciation for its attractiveness and partly because it seemed so easy to get to. As the road turned left toward the Kennedy Center, I thought how early we were going to arrive and how much time we'd have to look around inside. But then the road veered to the right and the Kennedy Center disappeared.

---

[11] John Steinbeck, *East of Eden* (New York: Penguin, 1952), 384–85.

Getting anywhere in Washington requires a remarkable sense of direction and a tremendous amount of luck. That night, I had neither. I wove my way around downtown streets hoping to see the building again before the intermission. Fifteen minutes later, I saw it approaching on our right. But this time, the road took a strange twist off to the left, and, before I knew it, my wife and I had arrived at Arlington Cemetery. After our third time crossing the Potomac River, we finally found our way to the parking lot and scrambled to our seats just in time for the curtain's opening.

As we sat down, I whispered in my wife's ear, "The Kennedy Center is easy to miss." We still go there. But every time, I pay careful attention to road signs and landmarks. Because it is easy to miss, I heighten my attention to detail and my sensitivity to possible mistakes.

In a similar way, I have found that the Scriptures teach it is easy to miss the gospel. So it is very important to pay close attention to detail and heighten our awareness that one small wrong turn can lead us to another message or some very different conclusion.

Think of the many places in the New Testament that warn us to be careful about our doctrine and examine our beliefs and choose our words carefully. Paul wrote an entire book, his letter to the Galatians, to rebuke them for "turning to a different gospel" (Gal. 1:6). He called them "foolish" (3:1) and marveled that they missed the truth and chose a message proclaimed by people who should be "accursed" (1:9).

In his letter to Titus, a mature pastor, Paul did not just assume this Christian leader was immune from missing the gospel. In three rather extensive passages (Titus 1:1–3; 2:11–14; 3:3–8), he restated the gospel message, showing how full and rich it is and therefore worthy of deep reflection and careful attention. It was as if Paul were telling Titus, "Choose your words carefully—both the ones you think and the ones you preach—for the difference between truth and error is no small matter."

It's easy for nonbelievers to miss the gospel too. They can hear it as a benign message about some vague love-force in the universe or a positive mental attitude that brings success. They may think their worst problem is choosing to live a shallow life instead of an abundant one, whatever that means. They'll interpret our words as mere suggestions for behavior that make their life better here and now. Many popular books reinforce this distortion.

When Jesus concluded his Sermon on the Mount, he warned, in one of the most disturbing passages of the Bible, that even some people who said to Jesus, "Lord, Lord," will not enter the kingdom of heaven (Matt. 7:21). In other words, people who thought they had found the gospel had, in reality, missed it.

When Paul preached on Mars Hill, he navigated that delicate balance between relevance to his audience and faithfulness to the gospel. He included what might be considered the attractive parts of his message (that God is our source of life and meaning, that he is knowable and personal, and that he is the one we are looking for). But he did not shy away from including some unwelcome parts of the message (that this same God will judge the world and demands repentance for sin).

Sometimes we so desperately want our family to receive our message, we overstate the attractive parts and understate (or totally omit) the unwelcome parts. Given the tilt in our society toward tolerance and positive self-esteem, most everyone will hear only the part about God loving them. "Of course, he loves me," they'll think. "Why wouldn't he?" Any notion of judgment or repentance will seem alien, to say the least. This kind of message may sound good at first, but ultimately, it may inoculate people against the gospel.

Implications for Evangelism

First, we must become proficient in the pre-evangelistic task of leveling the playing field. Many people feel intellectually and morally superior to us and approach spiritual conversations by looking down at us. They assume all Christians are simpletons ("Why else would someone believe such nonsense?") or bigots ("How dare they claim that their way is the only way?").

Rather than accepting this unfair playing field, we should level it. We should ask questions or make comments to show that both sides of the debate have valid points and both sides take aspects of their beliefs by faith.

Paul leveled the playing field when he began his Areopagus address with, "Men of Athens, I perceive that in every way you are very religious" (Acts 17:22). Given what we know about Epicureans and Stoics, that might have sounded ridiculous to them. They didn't see themselves as religious. They determined truth through reason and observation, not faith and superstition. But Paul wanted them to see that some of their starting points were just as faith-based or "religious" as his.

We need to do the same thing today. We need to show people that their atheism, agnosticism, naturalism, or any variety of unbelief rests on foundations that cannot be proven in a laboratory. We want them to be honest about their faith position so we can compare it with our faith position.

Timothy Keller models this well in his best-selling book, *The Reason for God*. In his introduction he urges Christians and non-Christians to admit their doubts. For believers, "such a process will lead you, even after you come to a position of strong faith, to respect and understand those who doubt." Skeptics, on the other hand, "must learn to look for a type of faith hidden within their reasoning. All doubts, however skeptical and cynical they may seem, are really a set of alternate beliefs."[12]

This is difficult but necessary preparation for a proclamation of the gospel. It can sound something like this:

You: I'd like to talk to you about your religious beliefs.

Your sister: Oh, I don't have any religious beliefs. I'm not religious like you are. I only accept things that I can prove rationally or scientifically.

You: But that sounds like a very religious thing to say.

Your sister: What do you mean?

You: Why do you think science and reason are better ways to determine truth than religion is?

Your sister: Because they just are.

You: Can you prove that scientifically?

Your sister: Can I prove what scientifically?

You: That scientific beliefs are more sound than religious ones.

Your sister: Well, no. I can't. But it's just obvious, isn't it?

You: Not to me. And not to a lot of other people either. In fact, it takes a fair amount of faith to believe in science the way you do.

Your sister: Are you criticizing me?

You: Not at all. I just think we have more in common than you think. We both accept certain things by faith. You have faith in science. I have faith in religion. I'd just like to compare our two faiths.

Your sister: I never thought of it that way. OK. Where do we begin?

Second, our substantive, line-drawing, illuminating, decision-prompting gospel requires the use of words. Actions are not enough. While it is tempting to just "walk the walk," your relatives may never understand why you do so. Sooner or later, you'll need to connect "talk" to your "walk."

---

[12] Timothy Keller, *The Reason for God* (New York: Dutton, 2008), xvi–xvii.

This seems obvious but demands attention in a culture that demeans the value of words. Some Christians love to quip, "Preach the gospel at all times. Use words if necessary." They attribute this slogan to Francis of Assisi, but it is unlikely he ever said it.[13] In fact, Francis used words rather boldly. One contemporary, Thomas of Celano said, "His words were like fire, piercing the heart." A church historian recorded, "Francis . . . [would] preach in the streets, the marketplaces, wherever people would listen. The gospel of grace was being declared in a fashion not heard for many years."[14]

Regardless of who said anything like, "use words only when necessary," we should reject it. We always need to use words! Don't be silenced by pious sounding gibberish about the "problem" with words. To be sure, we must back up our words with godly actions. *Both* make evangelism fruitful just as both wings of an airplane make flying possible.

A third implication flows from the second. Our confidence can rest in the self-authenticating substance of our message rather than in our ability to proclaim it. We can be bold because God's message is true. Even if we proclaim the gospel with "fear and much trembling" (Paul's description of his evangelistic efforts in Corinth; see 1 Cor. 2:3), we can rely on God to use it to change people's lives.

This differs significantly from the clichéd approach of "earning the right to be heard." People mean different things when they use that phrase. Some have a valid point that we can pave the way to greater receptivity to the gospel with expressions of compassion, patient listening, and gracious respect. But many people hide behind "earning the right to be heard" and never

---

[13] The closest Francis came to saying this was in chapter seventeen of his Rule of 1221. He told the friars not to preach unless they had received the proper permission to do so. Then he added, "Let all the brothers, however, preach by their example." See St. Francis of Assisi, *Writings and Early Biographies*, ed. Marion A. Habig (Chicago: Franciscan Herald Press, 1973), 44.

[14] Lewis A. Drummond, *The Canvas Cathedral* (Nashville: Thomas Nelson, 2003), 214–15.

get around to saying much at all. The problem comes from trusting in our own behavior that might earn the right to be heard more than in the power of the message. There are far too many examples of people who have responded to the gospel even though it was announced to them by someone who didn't wait to earn the platform to do so.

Finally, we need to choose carefully the tools we use to communicate the gospel. Books, tracts, websites, illustrations, and diagrams all need careful examination before use. Theological accuracy weighs in as more crucial than mere pragmatic success. Just because a book sells well doesn't mean it conveys truth.[15] Even though some people caution against "theological thought police," we need to consider a much greater danger. Given all that Jesus said about apostasy (see Matt. 24:11), it is impossible to be *too* concerned about theological accuracy.

If a so-called "evangelistic" book doubts the possibility of verbal revelation, we shoot ourselves in the foot by giving it to anyone. Even if it contains some positive qualities, we undermine the Bible's authority while trying to point people to the God of the Bible.

Or if a tract or online presentation of the gospel *only* refers to our sin as "brokenness," we are misrepresenting the truth. Yes, sin certainly does cause brokenness. But most people hear that word as something done *to* us rather than something caused *by* us. They think we are broken because we are victims. But the Bible's depiction of sin describes it as rebellion and idolatry. We must find ways to express that without watering it down.[16]

Since gospel-truth has substance, we should think deeply about it. Since it draws lines, we should stand boldly in it.

---

[15] I often consult two websites for help in discerning the theological veracity of a book. 9Marks (www.9marks.org) and Discerning Reader (www.discerningreader.com) have alerted me to good tools to recommend and bad tools to shun.

[16] Again, I appeal to Timothy Keller's *The Reason for God* as an excellent example of how to do this. See especially his discussion of idolatry on pages 275–76.

Since it illumines all of life, we should celebrate its fullness. Since it prompts a response, we should ask for one. Since it's easy to get wrong, we should reflect carefully about how to communicate it.

Steps to Take

1. Deepen your understanding of the gospel by reading challenging books that model theological reflection. A good starting point might be J. I. Packer's *Concise Theology*. A more advanced study could be John Piper's *The Pleasures of God*.
2. Read through several gospel tracts and find one that you'd feel comfortable sharing. Remember that theological accuracy is your highest priority. Beware of presentations that are more man-centered than God-centered. Wording, graphics, and tone are also important. One I like is *Two Ways to Live* (see http://www.matthiasmedia.com.au/2wtl).
3. Initiate some conversations about other topics that may connect easily to the gospel. At this point, avoid the more controversial ones like abortion or gay marriage. Asking about life-long goals, highest priorities, sources of hope, etc., may spark some good conversations.
4. Practice "leveling the playing field" when someone claims to have a nonfaith-based point of view. Try to show that all worldviews have some elements of faith. This will take several tries before you feel confident with this approach. But it's worth the effort.

LOVE

Always Craved, and Yet Seldom Conveyed

My wife's brother Bruce had not dated a woman in over a decade. At some point, you would have expected us to wonder if he was gay. At least one outside observer told us it was as obvious as can be. But sometimes, family ties blind as well as bind.

When we asked him point blank if he was gay, he laughed. "It's about time you figured it out. I decided not to come out to any family members, but if anyone asked, I wouldn't lie. Now you know."

Pam and I faced a difficult dilemma. Do we parrot the politically-correct lines our culture has brainwashed us to say when someone comes out to us? "Well, gay is OK. We know lots of gay people. We're not so intolerant as to reject you simply because your sexual orientation is different than ours." Or do we quote Bible verses about "abominations" and tell him he won't inherit the kingdom of God?[1]

---

[1] This topic deserves far more attention than I can provide here. I scratched the surface on how to witness to gay friends in chapter 8 of *Questioning Evangelism* (Grand Rapids, MI: Kregel, 2004). Other resources can be found at Exodus International (www.exodusinternational.org) and the National Association for Research & Therapy of Homosexuality (www.narth.com). Of particular value for Christians who have unwanted

While fully affirming all the Scriptures' teaching about the sinfulness of homosexual practice but wanting to keep lines of communication open, Pam and I attempted to walk the tightrope of grace and truth. We said to Bruce, "We're really glad you've told us. We'd hate for there to be any kind of barrier between us. We really love you and wouldn't want anything to ever hinder our relationship with you. But we think homosexuality isn't good and so we'd like to talk to you about another way to live."

He rolled his eyes and sarcastically said something about talking about that "someday." Even though we had received frequent visits from him up to that point, those visits (and phone calls and e-mails) came to a screeching halt. For the next year, we heard hardly a word from him because he knew our thoughts on his lifestyle.

Homosexuality presents only one of many painful dynamics that challenge our ability to love a family member. How does a Christian wife love her unsaved husband? How do Christian parents love their drug-addicted son? How does a college sophomore love his soon-to-be-divorced parents? How does a Christian sister love her newly-converted-to-Mormonism brother?

This chapter addresses two aspects of that challenge—how we understand love and how we express it. The two are inseparably linked.

What Love Is

We must begin by thinking carefully about the nature of love. This is not as simple as quoting John 3:16. The Bible's teaching about love is multifaceted and nuanced. Only after

---

same-sex attraction is Joe Dallas's *Desires in Conflict* (Eugene, OR: Harvest House, 2003). A thorough treatment of the biblical passages about homosexuality can be found in Robert Gagnon's *The Bible and Homosexual Practice: Texts and Hermeneutics* (Nashville: Abingdon Press, 2002). Exodus International also has several helpful books addressing how to love the homosexuals in your family. You might want to read those books before you get your first invitation to a gay wedding.

grappling with the Scriptures can we carefully begin to apply them to challenging family situations.

First John 4:7–12 provides a rich starting point for this process:

> Beloved, let us love one another, for love is from God, and whoever loves has been born of God and knows God. Anyone who does not love does not know God, because God is love. In this the love of God was made manifest among us, that God sent his only Son into the world, so that we might live through him. In this is love, not that we have loved God but that he loved us and sent his Son to be the propitiation for our sins. Beloved, if God so loved us, we also ought to love one another. No one has ever seen God; if we love one another, God abides in us and his love is perfected in us.

John has woven together a tapestry of the reason for love, the source of love, and a multifaceted description of love. Although this passage is brief and poetic, we can find a gold mine of truth if we take the time to unearth it and examine each gem.

The Reason for Love

This is not the first time John mentions love in this epistle, but it may be the most penetrating. The refrain "love one another" occurs three times, and the application for us to extend love in a selfless way pervades the paragraph. After the initial command, we are told the reasons we should love—because love is from God, because we have been born of God, and because we know God—all of which are undergirded with the profound announcement that God is love.

We can grasp how radical John's logic is if we consider what he does not say. He does not exhort us to love one another because people deserve love or that they need it or that loving others will make us feel good about ourselves. (To some extent, these statements have some truth in them.)

Instead, he says we love because God first loved us, because his very nature is love; we are now recreated by the gospel to reflect that love. We love because it fits our new identity in Christ and reveals the nature of the God who now dwells within us.

A rather complex reason for love comes at the end of the paragraph. Our loving one another actually clarifies to the surrounding world what God's love looks like. In fact, it may do even more than that. It may reveal God himself (not just his love)—the God that "no one has ever seen" (v. 12).

The effects go inward as well. When we love others, God's love "is perfected in us." I. Howard Marshall says, "When we love others, God's love for us has reached its full effect." He adds that when this happens, someone "fully experiences the love of God in his own heart and knows the presence of God with him."[2]

John speaks here of something far better than a dramatic mix of emotions or a stoic commitment of the will. This kind of gospel-love is better than either of those popular reductions. It transforms both the one who loves and the one who is loved. It displays and fulfills one of the greatest loves that could ever exist—the love of God for sinful people.

The Source of Love

John also speaks of God's love as a resource for us to express it to others. As we sense God's presence in us and his love for us, it simultaneously softens and emboldens us to love even the most unlovable people around us. This includes the ones in our family.

In a sermon entitled "The First Wedding Day," Tim Keller reflected on the nature of biblical love in marriage. He encouraged his hearers with this insight: "The main thing you need to really stick with a marriage is to over and over and over

---

[2] I. Howard Marshall, *The Epistles of John* (Grand Rapids, MI: Eerdmans, 1978), 217.

again look at your spouse and say, 'You wronged me. But my great spouse, Jesus Christ, even though I wronged him, kept covering me and kept loving me and kept forgiving me. So I am loved enough by him that I can offer the same thing to you.'"[3]

A Multi-Faceted Description of Love

John does not leave the term "love" undefined. He goes on to offer more of a practical description than a dictionary definition. Gospel-love differs significantly from the topics of popular songs and romantic movies. According to John, we can only understand love and offer it to others if we first grasp God's love for us. That love, divine love, takes the initiative, gives sacrificially, and satisfies wrath.

First, God took the initiative to extend love to us. "Love is from God" (v. 7), John writes and "the love of God was made manifest among us, that God sent his only Son" (v. 9). Just to confirm the point, he says it is "not that we have loved God" (v. 10). In other words, God didn't wait for us to make the first move. Indeed, based on other Scriptures, we *could not* initiate (see, for example, Eph. 2:1). If we are to love one another, it requires our making the first (and second and third, etc.) move. Expecting our unsaved relative to initiate love toward us *as a prerequisite to* our showing love to them displays the exact opposite of the gospel.

Second, gospel-love gives. It is costly, just as any inter-action with sinful people will always be. This is mostly an elaboration of the first point. When God initiates his love toward us, it is a sacrificial offering of his Son (1 John 4:10). But we must quickly move on, as John does, to see what kind of giving this entailed. We distort the gospel if we stop reading the passage after verse 9 and think of God's love with such trivial clichés as, "God cared enough to send his very

---

[3] Tim Keller, "The First Wedding Day," sermon given at Redeemer Presbyterian Church, January 4, 2009, sermon RS 310-1/4/09, www.redeemer.com.

best." (I've seen this phrase on bumper stickers and always wondered if non-Christians are supposed to think of Jesus as a Hallmark greeting card.)

Third, God's love is of a specific variety. John tells us that God "sent his Son to be the propitiation for our sins" (v. 10). Modern translations have struggled to find a word that communicates better than propitiation. The NIV chose "an atoning sacrifice." Opening his chapter on propitiation in his excellent study, *The Atonement*, Leon Morris writes,

> It is my pious hope that this chapter will not prove too heavy for the ordinary reader (and my private fear that this hope will be disappointed!). The trouble is that nobody seems to have been able to make propitiation simple. To most of us the term is just plain incomprehensible. Accordingly, it does not seem to matter much what it means and the result is a pronounced disinclination to make the effort needed to see whether anything much is at stake. But there is in fact quite a lot at stake; the concept is important for biblical religion.[4]

Morris defines propitiation as "the turning away of anger" and distinguishes it from expiation, which is "the making amends for a wrong."[5] I hope you won't dismiss this as mere semantic wrangling. These kinds of distinctions make great differences in the way we understand, live out, and communicate the gospel.

We bristle at the thought of anyone's wrath, especially God's. It sounds irrational or, worse, uncontrolled or sinful. We conjure up images of bizarre pagan gods that need to be appeased with senseless ceremonies or sacrifices. If indeed that is what John had in mind, we would do well to reject it.

---

[4] Leon Morris, *The Atonement: Its Meaning and Significance* (Downers Grove, IL: InterVarsity Press, 1983), 151. This is not an easy book for most people to read, but it is well worth the investment of time and thought. Morris examines the many words associated with the cross and broadens our understanding in ways that prompt worship and deep appreciation for the gospel. I highly recommend it.

5. Ibid.

But when the New Testament writers chose the word *propitiation*, they did so for good reason. It was a term commonly understood in their day. Wrath was not relegated to only pagan worship or emotional instability. Some evil was worthy of wrath, and the New Testament writers acknowledged that. A God who did not punish evil would not be worth worshiping. A God who punishes evil *while also taking that punishment upon himself* would inspire never-ending and inexhaustible praise.

God's wrath, in *both* testaments, flows logically from his essential nature of holiness and love. Because God is love, and because his love is the holiest of all possible loves, he must detest sin. In particular, if he really loves people, it makes abundant sense that he would hate any and every thing that does harm to his beloved.

When we learned that our son had gotten ensnared in drugs, I hated the world system that promoted those drugs. Far more than any amount of anger I may have felt toward him, I was flooded with love as I prayed for him to get set free. My anger at the drug world flowed out of my love for my son. (Consider the opposite: What kind of father would I be if I didn't care that my son's life had gotten so messed up?)

God's holiness is such that it pours out wrath on sin. God's love is such that it provides the One to receive that wrath. We must sense the full weight of both of these truths or the gospel becomes sentimentality or nonsense. Even if the word "propitiation" is never used in our world today, we must recover the understanding of it.

John Stott explains: "God loves sinners who are unworthy of his love, and indeed subject to his wrath. He loves us and sent this Son to rescue us, not because we are lovable, but because he is love. . . . No-one who has been to the cross and seen God's immeasurable and unmerited love displayed there can go back to a life of selfishness."[6]

Gospel-love takes the initiative. It sacrifices. It propitiates. To communicate and demonstrate this kind of love may be the greatest challenge we face in witnessing to loved ones.

What Love Is Not

We may find help in expressing gospel-love by considering how it differs from three common counterfeits.

Sloppy Agape

First, gospel-love is not "sloppy agape." It is not some vague, universal love people speak of when they say, "God loves everyone unconditionally." This fails to take into account that the Bible speaks about God's love in a number of different ways. Sometimes love is something expressed within the Trinity ("The Father loves the Son. . . ." [John 3:35]). Sometimes it is a providential love for all ("He makes his sun to rise on the evil and on the good. . . ." [Matt. 5:45]). Sometimes God's love is expressed as a yearning for all the world to come to know him ("Let all the peoples praise you!" [Ps 67:3, 5). This is the thought behind God's love in John 3:16. None of these three kinds of loves saves in the eternal sense.

God's elective love, however, is different. It only applies to some ("Yet I have loved Jacob but Esau I have hated. . . ." [Mal. 1:2–3]). Finally, God's saving love is reserved for only those redeemed by the blood of Christ ("He loved us and sent his Son to be the propitiation for our sins." [1 John 4:10]).[7]

---

[6] John R. W. Stott, *The Letters of John: An Introduction and Commentary*, Tyndale New Testament Commentaries (Downers Grove, IL: InterVarsity Press, 1964), 165–66.

[7] A fuller discussion of this important topic can be found in D. A. Carson's *The Difficult Doctrine of the Love of God* (Wheaton, IL: Crossway, 2000).

We must strive to clarify these distinctions or our efforts to evangelize our family and friends will bear little fruit.

I recently heard a sermon where the pastor compared the gospel to the end of the movie *Saving Private Ryan*. In the movie, Captain John Miller and his platoon save the life of Private James Ryan. Through extraordinary efforts, Ryan gets rescued, while several soldiers in the platoon die. As Miller takes his last breaths, he whispers into Ryan's ear, "Earn this."

The preacher then contrasted a kind of salvation that someone earns to the gospel. I eagerly anticipated what he was about to say. But his words missed the mark.

"Jesus is not like Captain Miller. He didn't say, 'earn this,' because we can't earn our salvation. None of us can. It's all by grace. It's freely given. We are all loved by God—not because we've earned it, but because God is gracious. God's love is unconditional."

Do you catch the problem here? It is not so much what the preacher said. It is what he did not say. His message of "grace" was too vague. It had no cross in it. It mentioned no wrath of God that needed to be propitiated. Contrary to what this preacher said, God's saving love is *never* unconditional. It is only granted on the basis of one very large condition—the condition of the cross.

The preacher's message would have been dramatically different if he had said: "Jesus is not like Captain Miller. He didn't say, 'earn this.' Instead, he said, 'I earned it! You can't earn your salvation because your sin is so bad. But you don't need to earn your salvation because I earned it in your place. It's freely offered to you because I paid for it with a great price—the price of my life.'"

Many of our friends and relatives already believe God loves them, and they think that is adequate for salvation. As a result, our pleas to them to trust in Christ seem pointless. We need to distinguish gospel-love from sloppy agape.

A Band-Aid

Second, gospel-love is not a Band-Aid. It is not an instant fix for complex problems. Forgiveness for sins is granted immediately upon conversion, but deliverance from the snares of the Devil may take more than a hug.

Many people make the observation that Jesus hung out with prostitutes and tax collectors, and then they smugly suggest that's all we need to do. They confidently add, "If we did that today, people would beat down the doors of our churches instead of run away from them." These critics of the church have a legitimate point that self-righteousness turns people off. Granted. But their romanticized notion of just "loving prostitutes" fails to appreciate the level of evil we need to confront and the depth of love we have to offer.

People tell hypothetical stories about loving prostitutes or hugging AIDS patients or accepting drug addicts no matter how messed up they are. They insist these people would respond with proclamations like this: "If there were a church that did that, I'd join it."

I wonder. They might come to our church once or twice if we told them God loved them. But would they keep coming after we told them they need a Savior? And would they beat down the doors if we told them to repent and "sin no more" (see John 5:14)?

Thousands of people came to Jesus when he was handing out free fish and bread. But he knew many did so only because they "ate their fill of the loaves" (see John 6:26). When he got to the part about being a disciple, many people "turned back and no longer walked with him" (John 6:66). What kind of silly notion makes us think that prostitutes would respond better than any other group of sinners? Some repent and stay. Some mock and flee.

I recently spoke to a pastor whose church attempted to reach out to prostitutes in their city. "It all seemed so hip at first," he told me. "Our people were almost proud of their 'out of the box' church—one that dared to walk the streets with hookers and invite them into homes for meals. They felt inspired by those who assured them the whores and pimps would stream into our church if they just felt loved by us."

The honeymoon of such naïveté wore off in less than two months. Reaching out to prostitutes plunges a church into a world far more dark and seedy than most anyone can imagine. The web of drugs, crime, and sex trafficking entangles people in ways that boggle the mind.

I am certainly not trying to discourage Christians from entering this kind of ministry. More and more of God's people need to do so. But it requires a clear calling so we don't quit when the going gets tough—which inevitably happens in just a few short hours. Such deliverance ministry requires perseverance, tenacity, and toughness that can withstand some of the fieriest darts from the Evil One. It takes a lot more than just hugging people and telling them Jesus loves them.

I doubt that many relatives of people who read this live their lives on the streets as prostitutes. But some may seem almost as far away from the gospel. We need to reach out to them in love. But we need a love with greater depth than what is often prescribed by well-meaning Christians so that greater deliverance can actually occur. Sometimes love is expressed with, "God loves you no matter what. So do I." But sometimes it says, "Let's get you into detox. I'll drive the car."

Stoicism

Third, gospel-love is not Christian stoicism. Many Christians think the godly response to loved ones turning away from the faith looks like a cool, collected, peacefulness that "just trusts the Lord." This doesn't sound like the Jesus who lamented for Jerusalem (see Matt. 23:37). Nor does it sound like the Paul who had "great sorrow and unceasing anguish" in his heart because of his fellow Israelites' rejection of the Messiah (see Rom. 9:1–4). Stoicism reveals an idolization of

115

one's own comfort and avoidance of pain. It amounts to an unwillingness to grieve over someone's alienation from the God who created them.

Dorothy approached me with tears flowing down her cheeks after I conducted an evangelism training seminar at her church. She pleaded with me for "something that will take away the pain." After asking what pain she was referring to, she elaborated. Her young adult son had walked away from Christ during college, and now, in his late twenties, was living with his girlfriend. He never attended church and seemed distant and cold toward his parents. Dorothy wanted to know, "How can I just pray for him without feeling so bad?"

I asked her why she would want such a thing. Why would she want to feel so cool toward her son? Is it even possible to love someone without ever feeling some pain? I urged her to stop praying a prayer she really didn't want God to answer. How tragic it would be if she stopped crying over a son who wants nothing to do with God.

Fred also approached me after a speaking opportunity. He felt OK about his daughter's wanderings. "I just can't be upset about it anymore," he told me. "She's a big girl now and has to live her own life. I'm glad I've gotten past all those tears and fears. I have peace and I sleep just fine."

Dorothy and Fred are not alone in their view that mature Christianity works itself out like stoicism—a kind of unfeeling happiness that can sing songs of praise no matter what's going on around them. I do believe we can sing songs of praise at all times. But I assume those songs often come with tears on our faces, lumps in our throats, and knots in our stomachs. Both Dorothy and Fred's responses elevate the desire for peace higher than the glory of God. Somewhere in between crippling despair and cool demeanor lies a balance of trust and compassion.

Rather than asking God to take the pain away, we should ask him to deepen our love. We should confess to him that some of our pain is really rather selfish. We long for our own happiness more than we want other people's salvation. Only when we get set free from a craving for painless living can we focus our prayers and conversations in ways that actually help others.

Implications for Evangelism
Expressing Love

Loving our relatives is a challenge. Expressing it is another. Family dynamics often create an odd tension where love is expected and assumed the most but communicated and received the least. I've never met a parent who said, "I don't love my child." But I have heard many college students, as they enter the stage of young adulthood, begin to wonder out loud if their father or mother ever "really" loved them. The facial expressions they have shown are painful to remember.

Gospel-love, by its essence, takes the initiative. God did so by sending his Son. We do so by taking the first steps. Parents need to find ways to express love so that their children actually *feel* loved.

I faced this challenge when our son Jon returned home from the boarding school where he overcame his drug addiction. The fourteen months he was away gave me plenty of time to soul-search and question whether my actions had helped him feel loved or condemned, accepted or shunned. Please hear me carefully. I am not accepting responsibility for his poor choices. I am simply trying to take responsibility for the essential tasks of fatherhood—bringing my children up in the discipline and instruction of the Lord and not provoking them to anger (Eph. 6:4), "lest they become discouraged" (Col. 3:21).

I had to admit that many of my spoken and unspoken communications to Jon had pushed him away from me—and my God. It was time to experiment with new tools. At one point in Jon's recovery, he told me how much he hated all the

117

rules we had made in our home. "Don't watch certain movies unless Mom and Dad approve them." "Limit the hours you watch TV." "Keep a chart to track hours on the Internet."

As he expressed his anger, two thoughts came to my mind. The first one was something like, "Well, if you want to live in my house, you live by my rules." The second one was much longer. An arsenal of apologetics started piling up in my mind to justify why I devised these rules, how our culture was going down the toilet, how I, for one, was not going to let my sons plunge down into decay along with all their peers, etc. In his mercy, God prevented my tongue from uttering any of these things.

Instead, I said, "Well, that obviously didn't work, did it?" Jon seemed stunned. I think I was too.

I added, "But I'd really like to find something that does work for you and me because I really love you and I want things to be better between us." It was the beginning of a brand new relationship.

If you were to ask Jon how he knew things were changing, he'd say it was when Pam and I stopped quoting Bible verses and preaching to him in our letters. Sometimes we communicate love by what we do *not* say.

When Jon first arrived back home, I joined him in watching episodes of *Seinfeld*. Previously, I never resisted the opportunity to express judgment on that show. It was too crude, too stupid, too pointless. It was, after all, "a show about nothing." While I still hold many of those opinions, at that point I thought it best to connect with my son without offering homilies on the decline of Western civilization. After all, there were *many* lines in that show that were just plain funny. For me to join with Jon in laughter expressed a kind of love he hadn't felt from me before.

We also watched all three installments of The Lord of the Rings. Jon loved those movies and had devoured not only the films themselves but also every minute of the behind-the-scenes interviews and director's insights on all twelve of the extended edition DVDs. Previously, I just urged him to read the books and probably added a few minilectures of the benefits of reading over the numbing effects of watching movies. Jon suggested I had the "gift of beating a dead horse." He was right.

Of course there are limits to what we can join in on. Many movies and television shows contain no redeeming qualities and may actually do harm. (See! I can't resist beating that dead horse!) But within the limits of wisdom and grace, we can pursue far more common interests than we might typically allow.

In his important study, *American Evangelicalism: Embattled and Thriving*, sociologist Christian Smith suggests that logical arguments alone cannot win all our battles. One of several lines of his reasoning states, "The primary basis of most peoples' distance from organized religion typically has little to do with cognitive belief implausibility, per se; rather, distance from religion appears to be generated more by relational disruptions and the absence of strong relational ties to religion."[8]

Perhaps this distinction can help: We need to love people simply because they are people, fashioned by God in his image; we should not show them love just as a way to evangelize them. Surely, we can find traits, common ground, unique gifts, personality nuances, and experiences we can affirm and, better still, enjoy. But we must not love them merely as a manipulative prelude to preach at them. They'll smell such nonlove miles away. Instead, we must ask God to enable us to love them. Period. No strings attached. If they're waiting for the other shoe to drop—a shoe in the form of a gospel presentation—they won't feel loved by us because, in fact, they're not.

---

[8] Christian Smith, *American Evangelicalism: Embattled and Thriving* (Chicago: University of Chicago Press, 1998), 172.

I can't tell you how many parents have said to me something like, "I just don't understand how my son could walk away from Christ. He's read a million books on apologetics, went to a great Christian school, and used to memorize huge portions of the Bible. Now his arguments make no sense whatsoever, but I can't get through to him. Can you suggest a book that would show him how he's wrong?"

These children probably don't need a book as much as they need an embrace. Actually, they need both. And that's the challenge. We need to communicate a content-rich message in a compassion-saturated relationship. We need to look our son or daughter or brother or parent or cousin in the eye and say, "I'm telling you all this stuff about Jesus because I really think it can help you. I'm not just trying to convince you of something that I believe to be true. I'm trying to offer something that I think can change your life. I really love you, and I want the absolute best for you."

Extending Love

God's love for us is sacrificial. Our love for others will always require giving. This includes adult children, who need to find ways to express love to their parents so that Mom and Dad actually feel it.

When I was a senior in college, I attended a seminar on "how to witness to your parents" at a Campus Crusade for Christ Christmas Conference. I expected the speaker to deliver some secret formula to bring my parents to the Messiah. The seminar room was packed with close to two hundred other eager students who felt misunderstood and underappreciated by their heathen parents.

The speaker began by asking us to take out a sheet of paper for a quiz. He actually wanted us to hand these in. Fortunately, he told us not to put our names on them.

"Question 1: How many times have you called your parents in the past month, just to talk—not to ask them for anything, especially money?" Groans filled the room.

"Question 2: How many times in the past semester have you told your parents you love them?" More groans.

"Question 3: How many letters have you written to your parents this past year?" (This was at a time before e-mails and text messages. Nevertheless, there are e-mails that imply, "Let's talk about me," and there are ones that communicate, "I really appreciate you, Dad.")

"Question 4: List three ways you express love to your parents other than with words." He looked around the room and saw blank stares on everyone's faces. I even heard someone behind me mutter, "Three?" He tried to prompt some ideas for us and offered the clues: "Obedience?" Honor?" "Helping around the house?" More groans.

I don't remember much more from that seminar. I don't need to. His quiz drove home all his points. Adult children often assume their parents know they love them. But that is a glaring omission. Especially for young adults who have been found by Christ and want to see their parents join them in that faith, expressions of love must not go unstated or assumed.

Expecting No Love in Return

God's love is propitious, an atoning sacrifice for sin. Therefore our love carries with it the assumption that people are sinful. We don't demand our relatives reciprocate our overtures. And we don't assume they'll always have our best interests in mind.

In some abusive situations, boundaries need to be drawn and maintained.

Carla told me of the redemptive work God was doing in her family. But her tone of voice was cautious. Her father had left her, her sister, and her mother when Carla was six.

For years, she never saw him. Mom moved in and out of several different men's homes, toting her daughters with her. When Dad did come back into the picture, it was for bizarre weekend excursions with his daughters. Often they went to bars, strip joints, and casinos. As a young adolescent, she watched pornographic films with her father. Carla recounted these memories with little emotional expression, except for an occasional nervous laugh.

When she went off to college, she heard the gospel and responded in a dramatic way. For the next four years she found love, acceptance, and healing in a campus fellowship. Now, ten years later, she serves as an education director at a church and focuses on discipling women from abusive backgrounds.

After many years of alienation, Carla and her father's paths are intersecting again. He has apologized to both his daughters for many of his past sins, and says he's looking to God for help.

"It's helpful for me to remember that my father is a sinner," she told me. "It's also helpful for me to remember that I'm a sinner. But I'm not naïve. I draw boundaries. I visit my dad in neutral places. He never stays with me and I never stay at his place. I limit our time together because there's still a lot of pain associated with him. I pray a lot for God to bring other Christians into his life so he can find the same kind of Christian love I have found. I need to remember that I'm not the only Christian in the world who can reach out to him."

Carla, I think, has found a healthy balance in showing her father respect and honor without opening herself to further abuse. There are ways to "honor your father and mother" without dishonoring yourself. This is no easy path, and I am not qualified to elaborate all the dimensions of this tricky topic. I can say that, on the one hand, I have met Christians from abusive backgrounds who still carry bitterness and resentment. In a sense, they are still enslaved by their abuser.

They need to apply the gospel's healing power to the darkest parts of their lives. On the other hand, some Christians naively think that "honoring your father and mother" must mean reopening yourself to further abuse. Neither option is healthy.[9]

Carla's insight, "It's helpful for me to remember that my father is a sinner," contains a great deal of wisdom. If gospel-love is propitious, we should expect people, including ourselves, to be sinners. And we can extend redemptive love to people who don't deserve it—because none of us deserves God's saving love. It will not surprise us when loved ones fail to return the love we extend to them. We need to build into our discipleship processes some training on how to love unlovable people.

This is especially necessary in marriages where one spouse knows Christ and one does not.[10] As I've read articles and books on this painful topic, I have gleaned several helpful insights:

- Don't look to your spouse for total fulfillment. Look to God for that. Even if your wife is a great wife, she's a poor savior. Even if your husband is a loving man, he cannot be your god.

- Look to the gospel to be the reservoir of love within you and extend that kind of supernatural love to your spouse. Peter's reasoning behind his command to wives to submit to their husbands is worth much consideration: "even if some [husbands] do not obey the word, they may be won without a word by the conduct of their wives, when they see your respectful

---

[9] The Christian Counseling and Education Foundation has several helpful resources for overcoming abuse. See their website at www.ccef.org.

[10] Much has been written about this topic. Careful discernment and scriptural reflection is needed in selecting which advice is best. One helpful resource is Lee and Leslie Strobel's *Surviving a Spiritual Mismatch in Marriage* (Grand Rapids, MI: Zondervan, 2002). Family Life Today also has helpful materials at www.familylife.com.

and pure conduct" (1 Pet. 3:1–2). Note that Peter makes no guarantees!

- Your conduct speaks louder than words—but both are necessary.
- Your hope needs to be in God, not your spouse's conversion.
- Don't offer yourself up as a perfect example of Christian faith. Instead, point your spouse to the perfect example of Christ.
- Build upon what you do have in common with your unsaved spouse. Find ways that the Scriptures inform and transform those areas of life.
- Devote yourself to extraordinary efforts in prayer for your spouse.
- Don't neglect your own spiritual life, especially participation in a church.

One careful distinction needs to be made. People come to mismatched marriages from different starting points. In some cases, two non-Christians married and then, later on, one came to faith. In other marriages, a Christian married a nonbeliever, fully knowing he or she was disobeying God's commandment against being "unequally yoked" (see 2 Cor. 6:14). These different scenarios require different approaches.

For both situations, the advice listed above, along with much that is written on this topic, will prove helpful. But in the latter situation, Christians need to repent of whatever idolatry led them into their current state. Only after the obstacle of their past disobedience is addressed can they approach their unsaved spouse with gospel integrity. I know this may sound harsh. But far too many marriages remain needlessly stuck at this point. The cross offers forgiveness for even this kind of sin.

Don witnessed to his unsaved wife with no apparent effect for over a decade. To be sure, he loved her. But he also had to admit that part of his motivation in getting married was fear. Approaching his late thirties, he wondered if he'd ever find a wife. He married a woman who said she loved him even though she had no interest in his Christian faith. He figured she'd come around eventually. Twelve years later, she still hadn't budged. It was only after Don admitted that he had disobeyed God, confessed it as sin, and experienced the forgiveness wrought by the cross that Don could witness to his wife with a clear conscience.

He didn't share all his internal processing with his wife. There was no point in telling her that marrying her involved some disobedience. But now that he had brought that sin to the foot of the cross, he could pursue his relationship with Christ with more freedom and joy. She noticed. The faith he'd been trying to share with her for years now seemed attractive. She has recently joined him in worshiping Jesus as Savior and Lord.

The motivations for marrying (and dating) non-Christians vary. But they're all bad. For some, like Don, it's fear or a lack of trust in God's provision or a lack of belief in the goodness of God. For others, it's lust. Other Christians find a kind of thrill in rebelling against their upbringing or church. For some, it's an indication that their faith isn't as important as it appeared. When you care more about a relationship with another person than you care about obeying God, well, nothing could describe idolatry better than that. In some cases, marrying a nonbeliever merely shows that Christ never was the center of that person's life.

These are hard sayings, and I utter them with great hesitancy. But until you get to the root of the problem, progress in your own spiritual growth will remain stunted and the likelihood that your spouse will find salvation is minimal.

Passing Love On
If we're trying to avoid sloppy agape, Band-Aid, or stoic versions of love, we might need to have some difficult con-

versations. Loving our relatives does not always result in harmonious discourse. While we certainly want to "live peaceably with all" (Rom. 12:18), we need to balance that with "speaking the truth in love . . ." (see Eph. 4:15).

As the only believer in her Jewish family, Rachel grew in frustration as her grandfather Lou advanced in years. Every time she broached any topic that could have sounded religious, Grandpa Lou cut her off. "I don't talk about religion—ever!" he would yell, shutting down any possibility of dialogue.

She asked me what she could do to break through to him.

"Ask him why you always do things his way," I suggested. I could see she needed both clarification and encouragement.

"Ask him if he loves you and if he respects you. I imagine he'll say he does. Then ask him why he doesn't ever let you choose the topic for discussion."

"He'd just tell me it's because he's older than me."

"So? Does the older person *always* dictate the topic of discussion?" I was trying to model an approach where the Christian refuses to accept a defensive posture and gently puts the non-Christian on the defensive. "Use the word 'dictate,'" I added. "It'll bug him just enough to convict him of his intolerance of your faith."

"I don't know if I could do that," Rachel countered.

"Sure you can. Say something like this: 'When people love each other, they both give and take. A real loving relationship means sacrifice in both directions. For all these years, I've sacrificed my desire to talk to you about God because you've always stopped me. That doesn't sound fair! If you really love me, you'd sacrifice a little bit too.'"

To some extent, I acknowledge this kind of confrontation works better in some ethnic contexts than in others. But you can find a culturally relevant way to express this kind of tough love. A gracious tone of voice combined with some tough words can express love in ways certain people need to hear. In fact, it may be the *only* way some people can hear.

Persevering in Love

Even though Pam's brother Bruce kept his distance from us, we never stopped praying for him and reaching out to him. In one of my letters to him, I included a copy of the boldly titled book, *You Don't Have to Be Gay*.[11] He gave no response.

After six more months of silence on his end, I read a magazine article about AIDS that truly frightened me. I wrote him another letter expressing my concern and included yet another book, Joe Dallas's *Desires in Conflict*. This time he did respond. The gay life had ceased to be thrilling and now brought one disappointment after another. He was ready to hear a different side of the story.

We restated our love for him, how we wanted the very best for him, and that we would support him no matter what. We listened to horror stories of condemnation from Christians. We tried to portray grace as something wholly other than self-righteous moralism. Mostly we spoke about what it would look like to return, after years of turning his back on God. Restoring his walk with God seemed to be a higher priority than changing his sexual attractions.

After a few painful attempts to reenter a church (I'd rather not repeat some of the foolish things well-meaning Christians said to him), he found a community of believers who extended grace to him. As fellow recipients of God's mercy, they could write their names alongside the list of sins in 1 Corinthians 6:9–10. While none of them practiced homosexuality, quite a few of them could wear the label of sexually immoral or idolater or adulterer or thief or greedy or drunkard or reviler or swindler.

Most significantly, Bruce started connecting to men in healthy, nonsexual ways. The way he describes it, "I had

---

[11] Jeff Conrad, *You Don't Have to Be Gay* (Seattle: Pacific, 1987).

to get my wires untangled with men before I could even think about relating to women." The process took years and included support groups, individual counseling, and a lot of encouragement from people who believed God could do the impossible.

Today he is married (*to a woman!*), plays delightfully with their daughter, actively participates in their church, and counsels men with unwanted same-sex attraction.

A few years ago, *The Washington Post* conducted a social experiment in what they called "context, perception, and priorities." They arranged for Joshua Bell, one of the finest violinists of all time, to play classical masterpieces at a Washington subway stop during rush hour. They wanted to see if anyone would recognize the world-famous virtuoso and stop and listen. They caught the entire episode on video.[12]

For close to an hour, Bell performed great works of the violin repertoire—Bach's "Chaconne" from *Partita No. 2*, Schubert's "Ave Maria," Ponce's "Estrellita," and more—on a violin handcrafted by Antonio Stradivari, valued at over 3.5 million dollars. More than a thousand people walked by without even glancing in his direction. A few paused for a moment, and several people tossed loose change into his open violin case. (He collected a total of $32.17. Yes, some people gave him pennies!) Only one person recognized the star who, just a few nights later, would accept the Avery Fisher Prize for being the best classical musician in America.

The *Post* writer and his colleagues had to admit their hypothesis was wrong. They had anticipated that, despite the stress of rush hour and the noise of the trains, beauty would transcend.

---

[12] Gene Weingarten, "Pearls before Breakfast," *The Washington Post*, April 8, 2007, http://www.washingtonpost.com/wp-dyn/content/article/2007/04/04/AR2007040401721 .html. You can also watch the performance on YouTube; search for "Pearls before Breakfast."

You can imagine how people interpreted this experiment. "We're too busy today." "We don't take time for beauty." "We have become musically illiterate." "We need more funding for the arts."

But Gene Weingarten, the *Post* writer covering the story, had a different take. He saw the problem as one of context. People expect a virtuoso when they pay large amounts of money to sit in beautiful concert halls where the lights are dimmed and the background noises are deliberately eliminated.

But in a *subway*, at rush hour, with irreducible noise, you don't expect Joshua Bell. You might not even want him! Weingarten concluded, "He was, in short, art without a frame." It was the context that shaped "what happened—or, more precisely, what didn't happen. . . ."[13]

In a similar way, we sometimes present our gospel-masterpiece in a context that belies our message. We speak of measureless love, unmerited grace, and infinite goodness but our tone of voice, demeanor, and lifestyles convey the exact opposite. We want people to quiet their hearts so they can hear the music of the gospel, but we're performing in a context of judgmentalism. We want them to feel loved by God, but they feel unloved by us. We want them to be amazed by grace, but they can't get past the smell of condemnation.

Perhaps we need to work on the context as well as the content of our evangelism.

Steps to Take

1. Make sure you are regularly feeding yourself on the reality of God's love for you in Christ. Pray the prayer of Ephesians 3:14–19 for yourself. Memorize and meditate on passages that speak of God's love, like

---

[13] Ibid.

1 John 4:7–12. Be sure to participate in corporate worship with teaching from the Scriptures, asking God to use those times to fill you with the knowledge of his love.

2. Identify ways you have attempted to express love to family that did *not* work. If necessary, ask for forgiveness for nagging or badgering your loved ones.

3. Brainstorm a list of ways you can try to express love in ways that will actually help your relatives feel loved by you. Different relatives will probably require different methods.

4. Try to discern if there has been a relationship that you have "given up on" (stopped praying about, stopped initiating, etc.). Try again. See if a completely different method of conveying love works better than what you've tried.

6

HUMILITY

Divinely Modeled and Yet Difficult to Find

I interviewed dozens of people for the research phase of this book. The topic of "humility" came up more often than any other.

Karen told me, "I wish I'd been more humble toward my mother. I mean, for crying out loud, she gave birth to me and raised me. But I badgered her about all the things she did wrong. I gave her grief for forcing me to go to a dead church. I wish I would have said a lot less."

Several people regretted saying too much. Hardly anyone said they should have pushed harder.

"I did a lot of damage early on," Bert told me. "I came out like gangbusters. If I had to do it all over again, I'd listen more and try to understand my parents. I just jumped in with answers to questions they weren't asking."

Many people regretted the foolishness of youth—spiritual youth, that is. When you're new to the faith, you're likely to come on too strong.

"I wish someone would have quoted the Hippocratic oath to me when I was a new believer," Greg said. "You know, the one that says, 'Do no harm.' That would have spared me a lot of grief."

Humility was a common theme in the good stories as well as the regretted ones.

"My wife surrounded me with believers," Ford told me. "She always assumed she wasn't the only one to witness to me. In fact, she got to say a lot less because others did the bulk of the verbal witnessing. I think that took a lot of humility and patience on her part."

Brian told me of the importance of showing respect. "I didn't respect my parents in the beginning and felt like I had every right to talk to them with a condemning tone. After all, they treated me like dirt. My logic was like, 'You did this wrong and this wrong and this wrong. I found Jesus anyway, despite your lousy parenting. So, now I've arrived. You need Jesus. You need to listen to me.' It was only after a campus minister rebuked me and told me I needed to respect my parents out of humility that I changed my tune."

Brian now serves on the staff of a campus ministry and says, "It's easy for the students I work with to think they have it all together now and they need to go instruct their family. But I try to tell them that respect is key. Go in humility. Thank your family for all that they did that was good and right and supportive, even if there are tons of other things they did wrong. It was only after I humbled myself before the Lord that I could do the same before my parents. And that's when they started listening to me."

Doris told me her witnessing to her Buddhist son (and his live-in girlfriend and their newborn baby) took a dramatic upturn when she stopped lecturing him about his moral choices and started offering to babysit. "It was hard for me to swallow my pride, you know, that he had rejected the faith I had raised him with, and also the values I had taught him. But he's thirty years old!" A steady stream of tears flowed as she talked. "At some point I had to give up the idea that *I* could change him. I had no control over his choices. The only thing I had control over was how I chose to express love to him.

And I have worked really hard to shut up and show my love. Our relationship is getting better and better. And, of course, I haven't stopped praying for him. We've even started having some good discussions about religion. But now it's like two adults talking instead a parent lecturing a child."

Doris also told me of her taking in her daughter and her two grandchildren after her daughter's divorce. Again, it was an opportunity to show love and not lecture.

Pain and suffering also recurred in these stories. When believers showed humility toward God as they dealt with trials, their attitudes spoke volumes to the unbelievers in their families.

The toughest story to hear came from Paul and Cecelia. After years of trying to woo their daughter to faith, they had resigned themselves to accept their daughter's pseudo-academic rejection of Christ. Raised in a Christian home, Ronnie went off to college and like so many, found intellectual reasons for skepticism. Her professors' attacks on the Scriptures sounded so much more weighty than her youth pastor's pat answers.

But then Paul and Cecelia's son took his life. Plagued by years of alcoholism, at only twenty-eight years of age, he despaired of ever getting sober. One night, in a drunken state of hopelessness, he jumped off a bridge.

If you were to ask Ronnie today what prompted her to rethink her parents' religion, she would tell you it was watching the way they worked through her brother's suicide. In the midst of overwhelming pain, they still found hope. While honestly grieving an ache that still, twelve years later, rises to the surface, Paul and Cecelia cling to God and speak of the grace of the cross. Their confident faith trumped any cynicism Ronnie learned at the university. She gave her life to the Lord one year after her brother's funeral.

Like the previous chapter's examination of love, this chapter's study of humility will look for insight from the

Scriptures and try to distinguish true humility from the phony kinds. The apostle Paul's pronouncement of the gospel in Titus 3:3–8 can serve as a good starting point. After exhorting Titus to remind his flock to take on attitudes of submissiveness, obedience, readiness for good work, wholesome speech, gentleness, and courtesy toward others, he offers a gospel-shaped rationale:

> For we ourselves were once foolish, disobedient, led astray, slaves to various passions and pleasures, passing our days in malice and envy, hated by others and hating one another. But when the goodness and loving kindness of God our Savior appeared, he saved us, not because of works done by us in righteousness, but according to his own mercy, by the washing of regeneration and renewal of the Holy Spirit, whom he poured out on us richly through Jesus Christ our Savior, so that being justified by his grace we might become heirs according to the hope of eternal life. The saying is trustworthy, and I want you to insist on these things, so that those who have believed in God may be careful to devote themselves to good works. . . . (Titus 3:3–8)

We need to follow the flow of Paul's logic. We can show humility toward nonbelievers if we grasp how gracious God has been toward us. Put negatively, we tend to underestimate how bad our sin is and then underappreciate how good God's grace is. Then we underexperience gospel transformation. Let's take this one step at a time.

On occasion, I have taught Bible studies on passages like this one in Titus. They contrast our identity before and after conversion. I have asked people to list three adjectives to describe their lives before coming to Christ and three adjectives to describe their lives now. The before adjectives people suggest include: confused, misguided, unhappy, empty, searching, etc. The postconversion descriptions include: happy, at peace, stable, satisfied, purposeful, etc.

I don't doubt these at all. But they fail to recognize how bad off we were. Paul wants Titus and his flock (and us) to shine the light of Scripture on our fallen condition and acknowledge its ugliness. His list of adjectives starts on the individual level: foolish, disobedient, led astray, slaves to various passions and pleasures. It then proceeds to the interpersonal level: passing our days in malice and envy, hated by others, and hating one another. We're worse than we realize!

Only when we acknowledge the extent of our alienation from God can we appreciate the depth of his saving grace. Note that God is the active subject in this passage. He saved us. (Twice he is called "Savior.") He washed us. He regenerated us. He renewed us. He poured out his Spirit on us. He justified us. Note as well what we cannot do in this saving process. We cannot save ourselves because of our works. To recall a similar passage, Ephesians 2:1–10, we were "dead."

And only after appreciating this death-to-life salvation can we go on to experience gospel-transformation. The "so that" phrase in Titus 3:7 shows the purpose toward which God worked this salvation in us. Not only are we declared righteous (that's what "justified" means), we also "become" heirs. It's a transformational process as well as a judicial one. George Knight comments on this passage in Titus: "The work of the Spirit in transforming and of God's grace in justifying coalesce in causing those saved to become 'heirs of eternal life.' . . . The 'heirs' are, therefore, those who are both transformed by God's Spirit . . . and declared righteous by God's grace."[1]

Because of Paul's frequent emphasis on the unmerited nature of our being declared righteous in Christ (our justification), some of us tend to shy away from speaking about our ongoing transformation in Christ (our progressive sanc-

---

[1] George Knight, *The Pastoral Epistles: A Commentary on the Greek Text* (Grand Rapids, MI: Eerdmans, 1992), 346.

tification). Rightly fearing a fall into works-righteousness and pride, we wrongly downplay the gradual nature of our growth. But this is to our detriment. We "become" more and more like Christ. This is a change of being, not merely a change of position. God's work in us had a specific beginning point ("regeneration") and continues to have a progressive process ("renewal").

To sum up by way of definition, to be humble is to see ourselves as God sees us in Christ—hopelessly sinful but graciously saved, rebellious yet redeemed, incapable of producing any righteousness on our own yet empowered to do all that God calls us to, appropriately bold yet taking no credit for the basis of that boldness.

Properly understood, biblical humility does not express itself as a kind of bragging about sin or a wallowing in how bad we are. Some Christians almost sound prideful in telling others how wretched they have always been and always will be. This fails to take into account that, by God's grace, we are being renewed and should show signs of gospel improvement. We should grow in our level of recognizing the depth of our sin. But that is not to say that we are getting worse. Scripture says, by the grace of the gospel, we should be getting better.

Remember the context of this passage in Titus. Paul is urging us to live with lost people in ways that show "courtesy" to them (Titus 3:2). (The NIV translates it "humility.") Only when we experience gospel transformation can we do so. If we fail to see how lost we were and how saving God is, we'll take credit for our salvation and push unsaved people away. If we fail to see our gradual sanctification as a grace-process, we'll lose patience with those who still haven't been saved.

As only a college freshman could express it, Talia once told my wife, "I'm trying to love my mother unconditionally, but she's making it hard on me." If you've ever felt this way, perhaps some meditation on Titus 3 could lead to the realization that "God loved me even when I 'made it hard on him'—so hard, in fact, it included a cross."

But don't equate humility with a lack of boldness. Humble boldness is not an oxymoron. In fact, we can proclaim the gospel both humbly *and* boldly when we appreciate its power to save people who are as lost as we once were.

After years of witnessing to her father, Cara finally asked him, point blank, "So, Dad, when are you going to become a Christian? What are you waiting for?" Sitting across the table from him at a crowded restaurant, she just felt like "the time was right." It was. Her father said, "I'm ready right now." Their waiter thought they were simply praying a prayer of thanksgiving for the food he had just served but, in reality, Cara's father was expressing saving trust in Jesus as his Savior.

What Humility Is Not

Finding good models of gospel humility is no easy task. In one direction we see proud Christians, incarnating a kind of arrogant religion we must avoid. In another direction we find non-Christians claiming to be humble, because of their "open-mindedness" and "tolerance." Sooner or later they show themselves to be anything but humble. And some disdain humility altogether, considering it a kind of weakness or psychological problem.

Despite its rarity, we must pursue and embody humility, for it shines beautifully in a world hungering for it. Just think of all the posturing and arguing that goes on incessantly on political talk shows. If anyone ever came across as anything but arrogant and obnoxious, their ratings would fall. But we dare not give up. Humility attracts people to the gospel, partly because of its refreshing rarity but mostly because it reflects the essence of Christianity. It was humility that motivated Jesus to leave heaven and it is that same trait we are called to imitate. Reflect on Philippians 2:1–11 and see the connection between Christ's incarnation and our meekness.

False humility seems to be growing in its frequency in our tolerance-obsessed world. Most people assume that anyone who would insist there's only one way to heaven must be arrogant. Conversely, anyone who sees all religions as equally valid must be, by definition, humble. But listen to these self-proclaimed humble people for a while, and you'll detect the intolerance of tolerance and the pride of open-mindedness.

I once read a collection of speeches and writings by Mohandas Gandhi, which all centered on his thoughts about Christianity. It was amazing how many times he told his hearers he was a humble man. After a while, it grew almost comical. I found myself wondering, "If you've got to keep telling us you're humble, it might not be true."

Many Christians exalt Gandhi to near saint-like status. But they need to reconsider their admiration. He misquotes Jesus and reinterprets standard Christian doctrine and then dismisses it all as something impossible to believe in. Consider just one instance when he freely admitted his unorthodox views of the faith:

> The message of Jesus, as I understand it, is contained in His Sermon on the Mount unadulterated and taken as a whole, and even in connection with the Sermon on the Mount, my own humble interpretation of the message is in many respects different from the orthodox. The message, to my mind, has suffered distortion in the West. It may be presumptuous for me to say so, but as a devotee of truth, I should not hesitate to say what I feel."[2]

Gandhi has many disciples in our world today, and I'm not just talking about the ones who acknowledge him as their

---

[2] Robert Ellsberg, ed., *Gandhi on Christianity* (Maryknoll, NY: Orbis, 1997), 19. See Gandhi's many other claims to humility on pp. 23, 31, 35, 37, 43, 52, 53, 55, 61, 70, and 102.

model. His spirit of false humility permeates and dominates our culture. The presumptuousness of those who think they understand our faith better than we do, attempt to convert us to a brand of religion that never seeks to convert anyone, and insist their post-Enlightenment, Western, secular faith is not narrow, needs to be unmasked. Not far below its surface lies a very narrow, intolerant, zealous form of religion. It is anything but humble.

The antidote, however, is not some form of Christian haughtiness, common as it may be. Just because we have the truth does not entitle us to swagger.

A model of humble boldness, for me, has been Francis Schaeffer, the Presbyterian pastor-turned-evangelist in Europe during the 1960s. His writings and experiences blend an intellectual engagement and evangelistic zeal with Christlike humility in ways that need duplication in our world today. Schaeffer used to speak of "taking the roof off" of people's worldviews as a component in pre-evangelism.[3] It is worth serious consideration and adaptation today.

According to Schaeffer, everyone has constructed a world-view that serves as a shelter against the harsh realities of our fallen world. The shelters he found while hiking in the Swiss Alps had roofs to protect people from falling rocks and avalanches. In the same way, people believe certain things—that God will accept anyone regardless of lifestyle, that our world is all there is, that God would never condemn anyone to hell, etc.—and this insulates them from grappling with the truly painful realities of life.

Schaeffer trained Christians to "take the roof off" by asking probing questions and taking people's presuppositions to their logical extent, thus showing them the flaws in their thinking. He would gently show people that their

---

[3] Francis A. Schaeffer, *A Christian View of Philosophy and Culture* in *The Complete Works of Francis A. Schaeffer: A Christian Worldview* (Wheaton, IL: Crossway, 1982), 1:140.

worldview could not stand. We need to become adept at this same skill. It is not necessarily an easy one to master, but it may be one of the most crucial evangelistic skills for the twenty-first century.

I have heard many people misquote Schaffer at this point. Instead of using his terminology of "lifting the roof off," they say, "We need to cave the roof in on people," or "We need to crash people's roofs in on their heads," and even worse distortions. It is hard not to detect some residual anger behind these words.

Somehow Schaeffer found a balance of boldness and compassion. He acknowledged how painful this process could be for the unbeliever. "It is unpleasant to be submerged by an avalanche, but we must allow the person to undergo this experience so that he may realize his system has no answer to the crucial questions of life. He must come to know that his roof is a false protection from the storm of what is; and then we can talk to him of the storm of the judgment of God."[4] But he would speak of engaging in this kind of dialogue "lovingly" and "with tears." If our primary motivation is to win a battle rather than to save a soul, we would do well to reflect upon the humility of Christ and the patience people showed toward us when we were "foolish, disobedient, led astray and enslaved."

Implications for Evangelism
How we humbly express the gospel to our relatives can be considered in three categories: what we say to God, what we say to our relatives, and what we choose not to say. Put another way, we need to consider the topics of prayer, speech, and listening.

Prayer
Years ago, our son David, who was only five years old at the time, was asked by one of his non-Christian cousins, "What

---

[4] Ibid.

does your Daddy do?" Even for me, explaining my occupational choice of "Campus Crusader" to my Jewish relatives poses some problems. After some thought, David said, "He's kind of a little missionary." That didn't help his cousin much. When David told me about this interchange later on, I asked him what he meant by "little missionary."

"Well, Dad," he told me, "I figured that the apostle Paul was a big missionary. So, you're just a little one."

For a five-year-old, that's pretty good logic. Actually, for anyone at any age, it contains some helpful insight. If indeed Paul was a "big" missionary and *he* asked for prayer in evangelism, how much more should we, little missionaries, depend on prayer every step of the way. When Paul wrote to the Colossians, he asked them to pray that "God may open to us a door for the word, to declare the mystery of Christ, on account of which I am in prison—that I may make it clear, which is how I ought to speak" (Col. 4:3–4). After all, this was the same Paul who approached the Corinthians "in weakness and in fear and much trembling" (1 Cor. 2:3). If Paul had that much fear and asked for that much prayer, is it any wonder we shake in our boots when evangelizing? Prayer can help far more than we give it credit.

I'm more motivated to pray when I think of evangelism as something impossible. Jesus told us "no one can come to me unless the Father who sent me draws him . . ." (John 6:44). He also told us, "apart from me you can do nothing" (John 15:5). I put those truths together and see evangelism as something that requires a miracle on both sides of the conversation. For my unsaved relatives to come to Christ, God has to work supernaturally to draw them. For me to say anything that can ring true in their ears, God has to work supernaturally in me. When I remember that, I pray more and rely on my rhetorical skills less.

Prayer is the ultimate expression of humility. When we pray, we deliberately take time away from "doing something" to just getting on our knees and asking God to do something only he can do. (By the way, praying on our knees helps our inward attitude move away from self-reliance. There's something about putting our physical body in the position of helpless dependence that prompts our inner soul to follow.)

In his excellent book, *A Praying Life*, Paul Miller makes the case that "prayer = helplessness." He contends, "God wants us to come to him empty-handed, weary, and heavy-laden. . . . We received Jesus because we were weak, and that's how we follow him."[5] He insightfully adds, "Time in prayer makes you even more dependent on God because you don't have as much time to get things done. Every minute spent in prayer is one less minute where you can be doing something 'productive.' So the act of praying means that you have to rely more on God."[6]

When we pray for the salvation of our family, we release them to God. We relinquish a prideful belief that their salvation is dependent on us. We admit that perhaps the only thing we can do is pray. Our prayers work in two directions—they pry loose our fingers from the control we thought we had on our relatives and they ask God to work in wooing ways in their hearts.

Our prayers for our family may steer us in directions we hadn't anticipated. What started out as, "O God, give me the words to say" may become, "O Lord, bring others into their lives who will reach them in ways I haven't been able to." Or, what began as, "Father, open their hearts to your Word," may lead to, "O God, help me to rest in your timing." Along with, "Lord, make my family receptive to your gospel," you might also add, "Father, make me submissive to your sovereign will for my loved ones. Help me to pray, 'not my will but thy will be done.'"

---

[5] Paul E. Miller, *A Praying Life: Connecting with God in a Distracting World* (Colorado Springs: NavPress, 2009), 54–55.
[6] Ibid., 49.

Speech

Humility expresses itself in a myriad of ways. The words we say can soften the hearts of our unsaved relatives while working a similar transformation in us. James said the tongue can steer us the way a rudder does a ship (see James 3:4–5). Why not choose our words carefully so we come across as ambassadors of a gracious Savior instead of as pundits for an angry taskmaster?

Sometimes humility is framed as a question.

Lonny grabbed the outstretched arm of his teammate Nat and stopped him from punching the lights out of the referee who had just made a lousy call.

"Do you really want to let anger ruin your life?" Lonny asked. The question opened up both Nat's fist and his heart. "I don't know how to live any other way," he confessed.

"I think I can help you," Lonny said. "Let's finish the game without any punches, okay?"

By humbly acknowledging his own struggle with anger and showing how Christ had begun a deliverance process, Lonny led his teammate to the Lord—right there in the locker room after the game. (They lost, by the way, due to the ref's bad call. If they had won, perhaps the opportunity to present the gospel might have evaporated. A humiliating loss sometimes paves the way for the gospel better than a triumphant victory.)

Sometimes the humble question is posed as a request for permission.

"Would you ever be up for discussing spiritual things?" sounds less threatening to some people than, "If you were to die tonight, how sure are you that you'd go to heaven?" A permission question accomplishes two things. It disarms the hearer of normal resistance because the question implies you *don't* want to talk about religion right now. It also opens the person up to your presentation at some later date because they gave you permission. The contrast yields dramatically differing results.

Imagine yourself in my position. One night at dinnertime (when else?), a telemarketer called and said, "Mr. Newman, I represent Such-and-such Aluminum Siding Company and we're going to be in your neighborhood next Tuesday. We were wondering what time would be a good time for us to stop by and offer you a free estimate on siding."

"Never," was my response. "Never would be a good time. And please put me on your 'do not call, do not ever call, don't even think about ever calling again' list."

But a short time later, I discovered that woodpeckers had destroyed the wooden siding on the back of my house. When I called a painter friend of mine to come take a look at it, he told me I needed—you guessed it—aluminum siding. He recommended a company who did excellent work. I called them and left a message on their voicemail.

Later that night (at dinnertime!), someone called and said, "Mr. Newman, I represent Such-and-such Aluminum Siding Company and we can be in your neighborhood next Tuesday. We were wondering what time would be a good time for us to stop by and offer you a free estimate on siding."

Do you know what I said? "Anytime! The sooner the better!"

What was the difference? I had given them permission to call me. In a similar way (I know, the gospel isn't aluminum siding. Every illustration breaks down sooner or later.), when we ask people for permission to share our faith with them, and they grant us that permission, the witnessing process goes a lot smoother. The request for permission expresses respect for their time and displays humility. If they refuse to give us permission, that's good for us to know. Our efforts would have fallen on deaf ears. When people refuse our offer, we can humbly go back to our prayer closet and ask God to change their hearts.

Sometimes we exhibit humility by the way we interpret the news. The commentary we express about current events or people in the news can reflect a humble disposition or a haughty one. That colors the way people hear the gospel from us. For example, when a politician gets caught in a sex scandal, we may be tempted to utter, "I can't believe he's so stupid. Did he really think he wouldn't get caught?" But we need to view these events through the lens of Scripture. Was the politician's problem his intellect? Or was it something else? People don't hire prostitutes, have an affair, or visit Internet porn sites because they're stupid. They do so because they're sinful. Their fleshly appetites have enslaved them. They need a spiritual deliverance not an educational lesson.

A humble person, upon hearing of a famous person's moral train wreck, could instead respond with something like, "I can see how someone could get seduced into that kind of mess. I think anyone, given the right amount of power and opportunity would find it hard to resist." A response of sadness without condoning the sin points to the cross far better than condemnation or boasts such as, "I'd never be that stupid."

Sometimes the difference between humility and arrogance can flow from tiny word choices. The use of the word "we" instead of the word "you" can make a world of difference. "We all need forgiveness for some things" sounds more palatable than, "You need to repent."

Another tiny vocabulary choice that makes a big difference is the selection of the word that follows "I'm sorry." If you say, "I'm sorry *if* I hurt you," it doesn't sound like a real apology. It can almost come across as an accusation: "Well, I'll say I'm sorry but this is really your problem. You're too sensitive." A much better way to apologize is, "I'm sorry *that* I hurt you." Better still, instead of "I'm sorry," try, "I was wrong. I should not have done that." Do you see the difference?

Some of the most humble words we can say are "I don't know." That three-word phrase has the power to work like a crowbar to open people's hearts to the gospel.

Scott's relationship with his agnostic father, Walter, took a dramatic turn for the better when he finally stopped offering answers to his father's demand for an explanation for all the evil and suffering in the world. Previous attempts to philosophize about cancer, rape, war, and birth defects all landed with a thud before Walter's hardened heart. He assumed that Christians were all know-it-alls and his son fit right in. Only after the attacks on September 11 did Scott humbly admit, "I don't know why these things happen, Dad. I wish I did." That opened the door for Walter to admit the same thing.

"I don't know" also works well for questions less severe than the one about evil and suffering. When we don't know the answer to any question people may ask, if we admit our ignorance and add, "I'll try to find out," it shows people a humble heart that's willing to learn. It also shows a servant attitude that is willing to do the work to help a questioner find good answers.

All of these suggestions for humble interaction stem from the root assumption that communication is difficult. Very few of us command the skills of communication well enough to presume we've always connected well. A humble spirit frequently asks, "Does that make sense?" or, "Am I understanding you correctly?" It also offers statements like, "So, you're saying . . ." or "Let me try to rephrase what you're saying, just so I can be sure we're hearing each other."

This style of communication also assumes that a conversation differs dramatically from a sermon. When a preacher stands behind a pulpit, before a crowd, preaching the faith, he needs to come across authoritative and bold. The venue demands it. But when we sit across from a searching friend at Starbucks, the tone, volume, vocabulary, and attitude all need to soften. A problem arises when we learn most of our apologetics from a sermon (there's nothing wrong with that) but need to express it in a conversation. Once we accept the distinction, we can adjust accordingly. If we fail to do so, we'll end up preaching only to ourselves.

Remember what Peter wrote about our posture in apologetics: "in your hearts honor Christ the Lord as holy, always being prepared to make a defense to anyone who asks you for a reason for the hope that is in you; yet do it with gentleness and respect" (1 Pet. 3:15). Note that this attitude starts with humility before Christ and culminates with the same virtue before people.

Listening

Many evangelism training seminars focus exclusively on what to say. We also need to consider how to listen. Writing about humility, C. S. Lewis said, "Do not imagine that if you meet a really humble man he will be what most people call 'humble' nowadays: he will not be a sort of greasy, smarmy person, who is always telling you that, of course, he is nobody. Probably all you will think about him is that he seemed a cheerful, intelligent chap who took a real interest in what *you* said to *him*. If you do dislike him it will be because you felt a little envious of anyone who seems to enjoy life so easily. He will not be thinking about humility: he will not be thinking about himself at all."[7]

I don't worry about the "greasy" and "smarmy" parts of Lewis's concern as much as I do about our need to keep our attention away from ourselves. The challenge to listen attentively, ask questions that draw the other person out, and show genuine interest and concern for others looms large in our fast-paced, multi-tasking, distraction-prone society. Some of us have had our attention spans so eroded that listening well is almost impossible. For the sake of the kingdom of God and loving our neighbor, we need to recover this almost-lost art.

---

[7] C. S. Lewis, *Mere Christianity* (New York: Touchstone, 1996), 114.

James exhorted us to be "quick to hear, slow to speak, slow to anger" (James 1:19). By contrast, many of us want to highjack a conversation so we can unload our agenda.

This is especially a problem in witnessing to family members for two reasons. One is because we're witnessing. The second is because they're family. Because we believe the truth and know our worldview is better than non-Christians', we grow impatient with hearing their stories and opinions. It takes supernatural humility in some cases not to jump in and scream, "Oh, please stop talking such nonsense and listen to some truth for a change." Reflect on some of the things you said before coming to faith (and after!) and meditate on how patient God has been with you.

We also want to skip all that listening stuff and jump to preaching because they're our family. We think we know what they're going to say. We've heard them so many times before, we can practically finish their sentences. (Sometimes we *do* finish their sentences and that really harms our witnessing capabilities. Ask God to still your tongue when necessary.)

When I conduct evangelism seminars, I spend a fair amount of time on listening exercises. I pair people up and invite them to have an unusual kind of conversation. One partner just talks about whatever he or she cares to talk about. The other partner is only allowed to ask questions. When I explain the "rules" for this process, I see many people roll their eyes and look toward the exits. I'm sure some of them think, "This isn't why I came to an evangelism training seminar."

But after a few minutes of this drill, I ask for feedback. Invariably, those who were only allowed to ask questions report how difficult this is. They all want to jump in and tell their story. I warn them to beware of telltale vocabulary that signals a hijacking of the conversation.

"Me too" is a favorite. They just told you they had a stressful day, and you want to tell them about yours.

"That's like . . ." is an even worse offender. They just told you about a great deal they got on a new coat and you want to trump them with, "That's like the bargain I got on my new hat. Let me tell you about it."

Nothing screams "I don't care about you" louder than an interruption or a hijacking comment that jerks the attention away from them and onto you. The solution needs to come from two directions—outward and inward. The outward solution is to train your mouth to not say certain things ("me too," "that's like," "oh yeah") and to ask questions that draw out further detail ("tell me more," "how did that feel?" "what happened next?"). Sometimes you can get people to talk more just by making a one-word comment ("really?" "wow," "amazing") or short commentary ("That must have been upsetting," "You must have felt great at that moment," "I'm so happy for you.")

The inward motivation for better listening comes from feeding your soul on God's overwhelming love for you. When your need for love gets satisfied from above, you'll demand less attention from others. You'll be able to love them, through humble listening, because of the love you have received from God. This is no quick fix. This kind of capacity for love is a by-product of many hours of disciplined meditation and prayer.

Healing Listening
One specific kind of listening deserves special attention. While the institution of the family holds potential for great love and support, it can also be the setting for horrific abuse. The very place God designed for protection and sustenance gets targeted by the Devil for the worst kinds of pain and violation. When abused children grow into adulthood and start remembering their painful past, a great deal of anger can rise to the surface. Many of these adult children point their anger toward God and vent it on Christians. If you're

related to one of these victims, it shouldn't surprise you if you receive undeserved abuse from the abused.

Counselor and author David Powlison says that victims of abuse need to know that recovery is possible. He has written several compassionate resources to help with the recovery process. He balances realism and hope with pointed advice such as, "you already know you can't just snap your fingers and make everything all better. And you know that pat answers won't help you. But here are two important truths to keep in mind: You are not alone, and there is hope."[8]

As someone who may get the opportunity to hear people process the effects of abuse, you will need compassion, wisdom, and boldness. The compassion can help you show empathy, listen patiently, and hurt deeply for the person. Don't be afraid to cry along with them or, to a limited extent, express anger at the sin perpetrated against them. The wisdom can help you know when to steer the conversation in the direction of healing instead of bitterness. The boldness can enable you to express concern that their "processing" of their abuse may be making things worse.

One woman told me that after years of hearing her sister give graphic reports from her many support group sessions, she realized her sister's entire identity was wrapped up in her past trauma. In a sense, she was *still* being abused by events that happened over twenty years ago. Powlison's insight that "your identity is bigger than your abuse" and "your story is bigger than your abuse" were the messages this woman needed to hear.[9]

Others have told me that a sibling's anger at God for their abuse simply served as a convenient excuse for avoiding the

---

[8] David Powlison, *Recovering from Child Abuse: Help and Healing for Victims*, http:// www.ccef.org/recovering-child-abuse-help-and-healing-victims-part-1 and http://www .ccef.org/recovering-child-abuse-help-and-healing-victims-part-2. This article is adapted from Powlison's booklet, *Recovering from Child Abuse: Healing and Hope for Victims* (Greensboro, NC: New Growth Press, 2008).

[9] Ibid.

convicting aspect of the gospel. As long as they could shake their fist at God, they felt justified in rejecting his offer of grace. In fact, their abuse *was* their justification. They felt they should be excused for any sin they may have committed "because of all I've been through."

Not all abuse recovery approaches lead to healing. Some people progress from denied pain to realized pain to analyzed pain to angry pain. But they're still in pain! I sometimes wonder after hearing testimonies of "recovering" victims if they've only gone from "I'm in such pain and I don't know why" to "I'm still in pain but now I can tell you why." Some of them can tell you far more than you want to hear.

At some point, after a good amount of sincere listening, we need to "speak the truth in love" to these wounded relatives and try to unglue them from their pain. It may take several attempts from a variety of angles but getting them to the point of healing and grace should be our steadfast goal. Our words can be crafted to sound something like one of these statements:

"I'm so sorry you had to endure such evil. I want to support you in any way I can so you can find the help you need. I think God can bring the kind of healing and wholeness you're longing for."

"I don't blame you for feeling angry. But I hope you won't stay that way for the rest of your life."

"I'm glad you're making progress on getting free from your past. I hope you won't settle for just understanding what happened to you. I'll pray you keep going until you gain freedom and grace."

"I won't pretend to know why something like this ever happens. And I'm so sorry that it happened to you. But you're not alone in this healing process. There are many people who have found answers in the message of Jesus. He, too, was abused, in some of the worst ways possible. Somehow, his wounds have helped many people get set free from their wounds. Would you ever be up for talking about that?"

As we humble ourselves before God, acknowledging our wounds as well as our rebellions, our hurts as well as our hates, we can experience a grace that washes us with rebirth and renewal. Then we can humbly serve as conduits of that same grace to others who need it just as badly as we do.

Two timeless photographs from the history of sports serve as contrasting images of evangelistic efforts in our day. The first is the famous picture of Mohammad Ali glaring tauntingly over his fallen foe, Sonny Liston, in 1965. Midway through the first round of a championship bout, one punch knocked Liston to the canvas. Ali motioned for him to stand up and resume the fight, famously yelling, "Get up and fight, sucker!"

I sometimes wonder if that depicts how some Christians view evangelism. "Go ahead," they imagine themselves saying, "Hit me with your best shot. Throw any question at me—something about evolution? The resurrection? Evil and suffering? Contradictions in the Bible? It doesn't matter. I've got irrefutable answers for all of them. Only a fool would disbelieve after they faced my arsenal of apologetics."

I overstate my case for effect. But after listening to some speakers and their disciples, I wonder if I exaggerate all that much. (I remember hearing one evangelistic speaker mock his detractors, saying that a certain skeptical theory "has two brains—one is lost and the other is out looking for it.") Perhaps that kind of arrogance helps boxers score knockouts. It has no place in the advancement of the gospel.

The other photograph holds staying power for anyone who has ever seen it. Derek Redmond, a sprinter in the 400-meter semifinal race of the 1992 Barcelona Olympics, fell to the ground as he approached the final turn on the track. Plagued by numerous injuries throughout his career, Redmond hoped for a medal in this, his final Olympic appearance—until his hamstring snapped and sent him crippled to the ground. The pain was so sharp and sudden, Redmond later said he thought he had been shot.

The entire field of runners completed the race while Redmond pulled himself up and started limping toward the finish line, mouth wide open with screams of pain. An unknown man jumped out of the stands to assist him but was stopped for a second by Olympic officials. Then, after saying a few words to one of the security guards, he was allowed to come up behind the runner and put his arms around him. One close look revealed that the unknown assistant was Redmond's father. Then, the two of them limped to the finish line, tears streaking down the grimacing runner's face, words of encouragement being whispered in his ear by a loving father. When they crossed the finish line together arm in arm, they received a greater ovation than the runners who had completed the race several long minutes before.

I like the second image better. I think it depicts the emotions and attitudes we should have in evangelism. In some ways (don't push any illustration too far), we are fellow limpers, putting our arms around injured runners and helping them toward the finish line of the cross. We humbly come alongside and say, "It's OK. Jesus already ran the race for us. His death could heal your wounds. He offers to forgive your sins. He's the one who can strengthen your weaknesses. Let me point you toward him. He's already rescued me."

Steps to Take
1. Write out the text of Titus 3:3–8. Then write out a list of the "we were" words from the text: foolish, disobedient, led astray, slaves, etc., leaving space in between to add your written reflections. Try to recall ways you displayed each of the words listed. For example, under "foolish," you might write, "that time I yelled at Dad because he came home late on

the night I needed the car to go to that party. I didn't care about him at all. I simply wanted the world to revolve around me." Then do the same for the positive words in the passage: goodness, loving kindness, mercy, washing, etc., and list ways you've seen the gospel bear that fruit in your life. The more you can "own" the descriptions listed in Titus 3, the more the gospel will transform you.

2. Continue to develop your system of prayer for your unsaved relatives. One idea from Paul Miller's book might serve you well; he suggests writing an over-arching request for each relative on a separate 3 x 5 card for each person. Including a verse of Scripture to "pray into" each person may also help. For example, if one of your relatives seems controlled by fear, you might pray the verse "perfect love casts out fear" (1 John 4:18) for her.

3. In the next several conversations with family, choose to keep the focus on them. Ask questions to keep them talking about their side of the discussion. See how long you can go before you're tempted to jump in with "me too" or "oh yeah" or "that's like."

4. Ask a permission question of one relative who might be open to a discussion. Word the question carefully to let them know you'd like to discuss faith *at a later time*. See if it paves the way for a better conversation than if you had insisted on addressing the topic right then and there.

5. Begin a few conversations with relatives about the topic of faith. Ask them to tell you their beliefs and find out as much as you can about how they came to their convictions. At this point, *don't* share your story or beliefs. Save that for another time.

6

TIME

Freeing and Yet Fleeting

Witnessing to family affords us numerous opportunities to live in tension. We love our family, but they bug us. We care about them, but we need breaks from them. They require the most patience, but they sap us of that very trait. We may need to witness slowly, but we feel the tyranny of the urgent. The luxury of time frees us to progress gradually, but the fleeting nature of time beckons us to press the issue. In all likelihood, we'll see our relatives again . . . and again . . . and again. But we wonder if we'll see them in heaven. With some degree of certainty, we assume they'll attend the next reunion. But with far greater certainty, we know they won't live forever.

It's enough to make us cry out for a formula. We long for a surefire evangelistic method to use with every relative in any situation. But there is no formula. I offer no timetables. Instead, let this encourage your heart: The God who calls us to live *in* time lives *outside* of time. We feel the burdens of deadlines, but he never does. We grow impatient, while he knows nothing of that weakness.

At the risk of sounding trite, I offer this: Witnessing to family takes wisdom. Knowing when to say more or when to hold back, choosing when to take the long-term approach or when to call for a decision, deciding when to build the case gradually or when to deliver the whole package, all come from walking closely with the Lord, depending upon his Spirit, and praying for wisdom every step of the way. Rest in this: God desires for his gospel to go forth. He longs to see your relatives saved. And he chooses to use imperfect spokespersons to deliver his perfect Word.

And all that takes time.

When my parents told me not to witness to my younger brother Brian, they were simply reinforcing his request. He had made it clear to them he feared my evangelistic fervor. After all, I had embarked upon the career choice of Campus Crusader. Of course, pressure came from both sides. He had good reason to avoid *anyone* who would talk to him about sin, righteousness, and judgment.

Brian drank his way through college. In fact, he got a jumpstart in high school. One weekend while my parents were out of town, he hosted a beer bash in our basement. When the crowd finally dissipated at three in the morning, he needed to dispose of the evidence of their festivities. So he collected all the empty beer bottles, combined them with the week's trash in two large plastic bags and transported them, *riding his bicycle,* to an unsuspecting neighbor's house several blocks away. (The visual image is amusing, is it not?)

Two days later, after my parents returned home, their doorbell rang. It was that unnamed neighbor holding two very large trash bags emitting the aroma of *eau de Budweiser.* The neighbor told my parents he looked in one of the trash bags and saw some mail with their address on it. That's how he knew where to "deliver" the message any parent would both want and hate to know.

College provided my brother with ample opportunity to advance his hedonistic urges. So it wasn't just my evangelistic zeal that contributed toward our alienation from each other.

Despite numerous invitations, he chose not to visit me for over five years. But then something changed. Perhaps my mother convinced him I would steer clear of the topic of religion or maybe he just felt adventurous. Or maybe God chose that specific time to work. One weekend he made the long trek from upstate New York to Pittsburgh to reconnect. For two and a half days, we talked about sports, politics, and women. We went to an NHL hockey game, ate a lot of food, and watched hours of TV. We laughed, reminisced, planned ahead, told jokes, and brainstormed possible Chanukah presents for our parents. We never came close to talking about religion. I considered the weekend a pre-pre-pre-pre-pre-evangelistic success.

Brian visited my wife and me several more times over the next few years. Gradually, he opened up to discussing spiritual issues. On one occasion, he complained that "I don't really know any religion. We're Jewish, but I don't even know what being Jewish is all about. I just feel totally ignorant about the whole topic of faith." I resisted the temptation to present a lecture of the varieties of religious experience and instead suggested that he might want to read the Bible for himself sometime.

Six months after that reading recommendation, the topic of faith took on greater weight. Our grandfather died. As Brian stood next to me at the funeral, he couldn't miss the fact that I became undone. I cried uncontrollably as the realization of Grandpa Joe's death hit me full force. I had tried to share the gospel with my grandfather (despite my parents' objections), but as far as I knew, he never responded. The horror of eternal separation from the God of Abraham, Isaac, and Jacob, the same God who sent his one and only Son, struck me in painful ways. And Brian noticed.

Sometime the following year, Brian came to visit again, and in total contrast to his first visit in Pittsburgh years before, he came with one and only one agenda item—religion. He

a qualitative statement of our conversion, not just a chrono-logical one. In other words, we should not only tell the "how I became a Christian" story but also the "here's what's so good about the gospel" story. We want to tell our relatives that the gospel affects the here and now as well as our eternal destinies. It's so good it makes us a better spouse, or parent, or friend. It gives us hope no matter the circumstances. It brings joy, purpose, meaning, and comfort. If we share specifics of how the gospel works itself out in our lives, we convey that the gospel is true *and* it is good. And that takes time.

Trust and Rest
If you're resistant to rest in God's timing, confess that as a lack of belief in his goodness or his power or his grace. Ask him to overwhelm your heart with gratitude for what he has done in your life. Repent of the pride that takes credit for your coming to faith because you were so wise or virtuous or willing to repent. (There is also an odd but common kind of pride that grovels about how sinful we once were.) Pray that God will help you find your rest in him, not in a loved one's speedy salvation decision. Perhaps the time needed to work in your family (to draw them to the Savior) coincides, in length and intensity, with the time God takes to work in your life, so you will relinquish control, quit making demands, and let go of the idolatry of placing people above God.

Time Is Fleeting
Let's face it squarely. Waiting hurts. In the course of gathering insights for this book, I spoke to parents who have waited for decades for children to come to saving faith. They recounted their stories with palpable anguish.

Marty scratched his head as he told of three married daughters who all love the Lord and one who does not. It makes no sense to him. "We raised them all the same, brought them to the same church, bought them the same books, hugged them all the same amount. But three of them married godly men and bring their kids to great churches while the fourth sleeps in on Sundays with her unsaved husband."

Edith freely admits she's jealous of parents of kids who have wandered away and then returned. Her daughter still wallows in the mud with the pigs. Actually, it's not mud at all. And that's part of the problem. It's tremendous success that keeps her daughter away from the cross. Decades ago, she ran away from home, got hooked on drugs, worked as a prostitute, and came close to death many times. Then she got pregnant. In a strange kind of way, the pregnancy "saved" her. She cleaned up her act, checked into rehab to shake the drugs, and opted not to abort. Now, fifteen years later, that darling granddaughter sparkles the love of God to her mother, stepfather, and grandparents. She's joined a youth group at a nearby church and talks to Grandma about the boy she likes who leads a Bible study at her school.

But Edith's daughter feels no need for God. After all, she straightened out her messed up life without his help (or so she assumes). Edith continues to pray for the salvation of her daughter. She's more than willing to let her granddaughter do the evangelizing. But it's been a long road, and every so often the pain bubbles over the surface, prompting her to shake fists at God and wonder what he's up to.

Perhaps that is why Paul told the Colossians to "continue steadfastly in prayer" (Col. 4:2). The terminology implies rigor and devotion. It takes more than willpower and a leather-bound journal. The problem with prayer is that it's easy to quit. The essence of entreating an invisible God to work an invisible miracle in a visible world sets us up for disappointment and weariness. Note that Paul follows his encouragement to pray with "being watchful in it with thanksgiving." When we pray, regardless of the amount of inertia dragging us down, we need to look for signs of God's work in the spiritual realm. We need to offer up gratitude for whatever we do see of his hand at work. An attitude of watchfulness and thanksgiving propels us to keep praying, sometimes through tears or even angry fits. Prayers need honesty more than polish. And they can contain seeming contradictions. So don't be afraid to utter prayers like these:

"Lord, I'm tired of praying the same thing over and over. But I will."

"God, it's been so long. Nevertheless, today is a new day."

"Jesus, I feel like quitting. Thank you for not quitting on me."

"Father, I see your hand at work. I just wish it would work in my son."

"I do believe. Help me in my unbelief."

Some parents make the waiting even more difficult, using Proverbs 22:6 to heap on guilt. The text says, "Train up a child in the way he should go; even when he is old he will not depart from it." It sounds like an ironclad guarantee that if parents do a good job in the formative years, children will never stray. Or, if they do, it won't last forever.

Some try to soften the blow by appealing to a minority interpretation of the Proverb. Since a literal translation of the Hebrew could be, "Train up a child according to his way . . . ," they see this as a mandate to adapt childrearing to the particular child's bent or personality. Any parent with more than one child knows you can't use the same parenting tactics for all children. One child will fight back. Another will wilt at the slightest correction. One will try to please. Another will rebel. You must adapt your parenting to each child. Of course there is great wisdom in this. But I am not convinced the text of Proverbs 22:6 is the place to find it.

First, the Hebrew probably doesn't support the translation "according to his way." There are valid reasons translators have used phrases like "the right path" (NLT), "the right way" (NRSV), and "the way he should go" (NASB, NIV, and

ESV).[1] Secondly, logic does not support this interpretation. Wouldn't children maintain their unique personalities in old age regardless of their upbringing? If a parent didn't train up a child "according to his way," would that child alter his or her personality because of that bad training? Would a combative personality morph into a compliant one if parents failed to adapt their training accordingly? The proverb, especially the second half, seems pointless if it refers to children's differing bents.

More likely, we can properly understand the proverb by remembering the nature of Hebrew poetry and the genre of Proverbs. A proverb is not a promise. Old Testament scholar Tremper Longman says, "Proverbs express ideas commonly accepted as true."[2] Another eminent scholar, Bruce Waltke, says about this specific verse, "The proverb, however, must not be pushed to mean that the educator is ultimately responsible for the youth's entire moral orientation."[3] In other words, proverbs are wise statements about how life *typically* works. They are not promises that hold true without exception.

Perhaps an English equivalent can shed light on this. The saying, "A stitch in time saves nine" is true and helpful for living life skillfully. It teaches us to take care of problems before they get worse. But is this *always* the case? Aren't there times when some problems don't get worse or just take care of themselves? Aren't there other times when the one-to-nine ratio is an exaggeration? Or woefully inadequate? To press a proverb so literally and universally misinterprets the genre of a proverb.

You can find numerous proverbs in the Bible that are generally true and worthy of serious application in daily life. But exceptions to their rule can easily be found without

---

[1] For fuller explanations of the technical linguistic arguments, see Tremper Longman, *Proverbs* (Grand Rapids, MI: Baker, 2006), 404–5; and Bruce Waltke, *The Book of Proverbs, chapters 15–31* (Grand Rapids, MI: Eerdmans, 2005), 203–5.

[2] Longman, *Proverbs*, 31.

[3] Waltke, *Proverbs*, 206.

negating its truthfulness. One need look no further than one verse away in Proverbs 22:5. The text says, "In the paths of the wicked lie thorns and snares, but he who guards his soul stays far from them" (NIV). Really? Don't we all know some "wicked" people who never seem to find thorns and snares? Didn't Asaph, in Psalm 73, bemoan the fact that he saw exceptions to this proverb all around him? Or go just one verse above. The text of Proverbs 22:4 says, "Humility and fear of the LORD bring wealth and honor and life" (NIV). Really? Don't we all know some remarkably humble people who fear the Lord but who never find wealth and honor? Haven't we known such people who die young?

These exceptions, however, do not disprove the validity of the proverb. They merely show that a proverb is not a promise or a universal guarantee. Hence, we should heed the warning to "train up a child in the way he should go" with great expectation that "when he is old he will not depart from it." When that does happen, we can rejoice, thank God, and enjoy the fruit that comes from generational blessing. We can delight that our children are spared the tragic consequences of riotous living. But we should not presume upon it. If we do, we're likely to take credit if our kids turn out well or heap crippling guilt upon ourselves if they don't.

Another way parents misuse Proverbs 22:6 is by passively sitting and waiting for wayward children to come back because, after all, the Bible "promises" they will. This attitude may reveal our demand for comfort rather than our dependence upon God. We need to apply the grace of forgiveness to ourselves if, in fact, we have not excelled in training up our children in the way they should go and rely on God's strength to remain steadfast in prayer for them until they return. Or we may need to humbly accept that we cannot control our children, no matter how great our parenting skills were. We live in a treacherous world, and some of our kids get sucked into evil beyond belief.

If indeed our children stray from the faith, perhaps they never really embraced it. In some instances, we may need to stop calling them to "return" to a faith they appeared to have. Instead, we should point them to a faith they may have never embraced. This may be the most painful discernment process a parent can engage in. But it may be the most helpful. Instead of wrestling with the difficult question of, "Is my child really saved?" it may be better to highlight for him the ways the gospel is different from common distortions of it.

No one-size-fits-all explanation can apply to every child's rebellion. Perhaps they're abandoning a message no one should believe. They may think the gospel is oppressive, boring, irrelevant, or arrogant. We should applaud their rejection of that kind of religion. Clarifying how the gospel of grace is the exact antithesis of those false faiths should replace our nagging to come back to childhood experiences that obviously didn't take.

When our son Jon went off to college, he wanted nothing to do with God or our religion, which he saw as a set of ridiculous rules. Pam and I sent him off with great fear and trembling—and much prayer. He had kicked his drug habit and expressed to us he intended to stay clean in college. He told his older brothers, both of whom were in college at the time, that he didn't want to get involved in any Christian fellowships but would choose friends who didn't drink or do drugs. Both brothers laughed at him. "You won't find any such friends except in Christian fellowships. And even there, there's no guarantee," they warned.

So Jon went to the Campus Crusade meetings not to find God but to stay clean. And the students there befriended him regardless of his lack of interest in God. One night he told Pam and me on the phone, "I signed up to go to a Bible study. [Pause.] But don't get your hopes up." A few weeks later, we heard about his introduction at the Bible study. He told the other ten freshmen that he didn't know what he believed anymore. He told of his recent fourteen-month stint in a "lockdown facility for troubled teens." Wouldn't you have loved to have been a fly on the wall in that dorm room? His fellow students responded with grace and acceptance.

Several months later, Jon asked for some money to pay for a Christian retreat. I have never enjoyed writing a check so much! Sometime after that retreat, he phoned us and said, "I rededicated my life to God." When Pam and I hung up the phone, I looked at her and asked, "Did that just really happen?" Our two-year journey into "prodigal parenthood" seemed to be coming to an end. We still pinch ourselves to make sure it's not all a dream. But we have talked to enough friends who are still waiting after two decades, not two years, and we wonder, "Why are we so favored?" Why God works quickly in some instances and seemingly not at all in others is something none of us should dare to attempt to explain.

Implications for Evangelism

If taking the slow route seems wise for witnessing to some outside your family, it may be brilliant for those inside. Several people have told me they accomplished more by attempting less when it came to conveying the gospel to loved ones. I'm not sure why that is true. Is it that "familiarity breeds contempt"? Or do we need to heed Ben Franklin's axiom, "Fish and visitors smell in three days" and space out our gospel conversations? If you do decide to pursue the gradual approach, try to keep in mind two illustrations—an alphabet chart and a standard transmission. Let's look at them one at a time.

A to Z

All my elementary school classrooms had charts of the alphabet on their front walls. From left to right, the alphabet progressed from A to Z. Imagine that the A-to-Z scale depicts a spectrum of unbelief from the most hardened, militant atheist (on the left at letter *A*) to someone ready to place their trust in Christ (on the right at letter *Z*). Someone at A loves to quote the new atheists while someone at Z says, "Look, water! What prevents me from being baptized?"

We all want to move loved ones to letter *Z*. We want to ask, "Would you like to receive Christ right now as your Lord and Savior?" and hear them say, "Why, of course. Why haven't you asked me this before?" And, God willing, we will enjoy that interchange some day. But if we're talking to someone far from a point of decision, perhaps at letter *D*, we might need a better tactic.

I think many of us received training in evangelism that assumed all our conversations would begin at letter *T*. Fifty years ago, many Americans were indeed at letter *T*, and you could begin an evangelistic conversation with the question, "If you were to die tonight and stand before God and he were to ask you why he should let you into heaven, what would you say?" That's a great question for people at letter *T*. They already believe in a personal God who would ask such a question. They already believe in heaven and assume some people will go there and some will not.

But our culture has shifted, spiritually speaking, in rather dramatic ways. Most people in America today are *not* at letter *T*. Many other cultures around the world have gone the same route. Some cultures have never had a majority at letter *T* and are still mostly stuck around letter *D*. When you ask a question that is appropriate for a letter *T* to someone who is at letter *D*, you might just as well be speaking a foreign language. When most of my relatives hear a question that begins with "If you were to die tonight," they run! "Why are you Christians so obsessed with death all the time?" they might blurt out. Or they might interrupt with, "Are you trying to sell me life insurance?"

I am trying to encourage different approaches for different people. Just as the apostle Paul became "all things to all people, that by all means [he] might save some" (1 Cor. 9:22), we need a variety of starting points and a willingness to progress incrementally.

By the way, I am not saying that God cannot move someone from letter *D* to letter *Z* in one conversation. He can. And on occasion he does. I am not implying any limitation in his power to save. But most often, in our day and culture, it takes time for people to move from *D* to *Z*. The whole process requires patience, to be sure, but it also takes a listening ear. We may assume someone is at letter *D* and ask them something like, "Do you ever think much about spiritual things?" But their answer may tell us they, in fact, are really at letter *Y*. They may respond, "Why yes. In fact, I've been reading the Bible a lot lately and I'm thinking quite seriously about becoming a Christian." If so, forget the gradual, slow approach. Get this guy to a body of water and start singing "Just as I Am."

It would be a worthwhile exercise to brainstorm some questions for a wide range of starting points and memorize a handful you could employ in evangelism. I'll prime the pump with a few:[4]

At letter *T*:

"If you were to die tonight, how sure are you that you'd go to heaven?"

"Can I show you this booklet [or outline or diagram or chart] that explains how you can have a personal relationship with God?"

"What is preventing you from becoming a Christian right now?"

"Are there any dangling questions you need to have answered that block the way for your giving your life over to God?"

---

[4] There are entire books filled with these kinds of questions. One I find particularly helpful is Gary Poole's *The Complete Book of Questions* (Grand Rapids, MI: Zondervan, 2003).

At letter *D*:

"Do you ever think much about spiritual things?"

"What kinds of things do you like to do in your free time?"

"What's your favorite book? Or movie? Or song?"

(For these last two questions, you'll want to see if there's something in their answer that tells you how they think about the important questions of life. If their favorite book or movie addresses death or meaning or some other transcendent topic, pursue their line of thinking and ask the Lord to guide the conversation from the movie to the gospel. This might take months! If their favorite movie is *Dumb and Dumber*, I'm not sure what to suggest.)

At letter *L*:

"Who has influenced your thinking the most about important issues of life?"

"If you had to sum up your philosophy of life in a few short sentences, what would you say?"

"Have you ever read . . . ?

(You can choose a book that lands anywhere on the spectrum from *A* to *Z*, depending on where you think the person is. For someone closer to *A*, it might be a novel written by a non-Christian, like John Steinbeck's *East of Eden*. Although Steinbeck had no intention of pointing readers to Jesus, his book raises numerous questions about virtue, sin, life, death, forgiveness, etc. So do novels by Dickens, Dostoyevsky, and many others.

Or you might ask about something more directly evangelistic like Timothy Keller's *The Reason for God*. If you always ask about Christian books, they'll see you coming and avoid you like the plague. But choose wisely. Just because something is a bestseller doesn't mean it contains good theology. In fact, if it *is* a bestseller, that might be a bad sign.)

One more thought. Age trumps alphabet. In other words, if your aging grandfather is close to death (how could he not be?), you might just want to skip to the questions appropriate for letter *T*—or *Y*! The time for subtlety has long past.

The Standard Transmission

If you've ever driven a car with a standard transmission, you know how important it is to step on the clutch before shifting gears. If you forget to do so, the gears will grind together, possibly causing permanent damage to the car. Something has to open the way for the gears to move properly. In a similar way, sometimes we need to engage an idea or dismantle an argument or challenge a prejudice or expose an insincerity before we can move forward with a gospel presentation. Until we do, our preaching about God or the cross or sin or hell will just sound like grinding gears.

Allow me to offer some suggestions of "clutches" we need to engage before shifting gears to our gospel presentations. Perhaps you can think of a few more that fit your family's situation.

The Clutch of Sincerity

The prompt: Your cousin Allen sarcastically says, "So I suppose you believe the same nonsense that hateful preacher believes that "God hates fags."

The grinding gear shift to avoid: "Well, Allan, the Bible does say that homosexuals will not enter the kingdom of heaven."

The clutch to insert: "Allan, is this a real question? Do you really want to discuss homosexuality or is this just a jab at me?"

The Clutch of Timing

The prompt: Your uncle Tony chooses Thanksgiving dinner (when your whole extended family is talking about how moist the turkey is) to stop all the individual conversations and announce, "So, tell me, Mr. Religious Guy, do you think I'm going to hell because I don't believe what you believe?"

The grinding gear to avoid: "Well, Uncle Tony, have you been born again? Because if you haven't, do you know what Jesus said to Nicodemus?"

The clutch to insert: "Do you really want to discuss this right now? With everyone eavesdropping? Why are you asking me such a personal question in front of everyone else?" Turning to the whole table, "How many of you want Uncle Tony and me to have a religious debate right now?" (Of course, there is the risk that everyone will vote in the affirmative and then you're in the spotlight. But even if it does go that way, your clutch of timing has probably paved the way for a better conversation.)

The Clutch of an Apology

The prompt: Your sister shacked up with some guy you didn't like for years before marrying him. It was her third marriage, and you were tired of buying gifts and getting dressed up for something you thought wouldn't last. So you didn't go to her wedding and there's been a rift between you ever since. You're pretty sure this has crippled any possibility of witnessing to her. Now, ten years later, she's still married to that husband, and you'd like to connect on a deeper level.

The grinding gear to avoid: "The reason I didn't come to your wedding is because your track record made me wonder if this one was going to last. I still wonder but I wish you the best."

The clutch to insert: "I've been thinking a lot about our relationship and I wish it could be better. My guess is that my not coming to your wedding all those years ago really hurt our chances to be close. I want you to know that I regret that decision. I wish I would have come to your wedding. I hope you'll be able to forgive me. I really want the best for you. I'd like us to be close."

The Clutch of Buying Some Time
The prompt: Your brother is much smarter than you and can back you into a corner with his quick mind and sharp tongue. He poses questions you can't answer and makes you feel like an idiot.

The grinding gear to avoid: "Oh yeah? Well, how about this?" (Then you try to stump him with a question that's unrelated to the one he posed.)

The clutch to insert:

Option 1: "You know, I think you've raised a good question. And I don't know the answer. Can you give me some time to do some research?" If he's not willing to grant you that, his question never was sincere. If that's the case, it's time to insert the clutch of sincerity.

Option 2: "Do you remember the other day when you asked me . . . ? I didn't know what to say at the time. I don't think as quickly on my feet as you do. But I've done some thinking about your question. Would you like to hear what I've come up with?"

The Clutch of Maybe
The prompt: Your son comes home from college with a barrage of attacks on the Bible—probably inspired by his religion professor. He says that nobody (i.e., nobody "intelligent") believes the Bible got transmitted to us without a boatload of errors. With all the translation and all the time, we just can't trust our Bibles.

The grinding gear to avoid: Handing him the latest apologetics tome or telling him boring stories about the Dead Sea Scrolls.

The clutch to insert: "Well, maybe. The Bible might have gotten distorted throughout time. But, on the other hand, maybe it didn't. If there really is a God who wanted to communicate to people, isn't it possible that he could get people to write it and translate it in some way that didn't get messed up? Isn't that at least possible?"

The Clutch of Concern
The prompt: Your brother drinks too much.

The grinding gears to avoid: Nagging, hinting, joking, ignoring, joining in on the revelry, quoting Ephesians 5:18 ("Do not get drunk with wine . . .") or numerous proverbs.

The clutch to insert: "Let's talk about the elephant in the room. I'm concerned about how much you drink. If it doesn't ruin your marriage, it's bound to destroy your liver. It's already alienated me from you. I think you need some help." (This is a much bigger issue than I can address here. There are some very helpful resources available about addictions of all kinds. Avail yourself of them and don't think the problem is just going to evaporate.)

The Clutch of Growing Up
The prompt: Now that you and your siblings are in your forties, you'd like to treat each other as adults. Remarkably, you don't. Whenever you get together, you seem to resort to adolescent behavior and old patterns.

The grinding gear to avoid: Just changing the way you treat them without identifying the root problem.

The clutch to insert: "I think we need to acknowledge that when we get together, we tend to revert to our childhood— at least in the ways we interact with each other. I'd like to change that, wouldn't you?"

In the course of his conversation with Nicodemus, Jesus compared being born again to the wind. He said, "Do not marvel that I said to you, 'You must be born again.' The wind blows where it wishes, and you hear its sound, but you do not know where it comes from or where it goes. So it is with everyone who is born of the Spirit" (John 3:7–8). In a poetic way, Nicodemus himself serves as an example of that wind-like work of God's Spirit. This ruler of the Jews shows up three times in John's Gospel. He first comes to Jesus "at night" (John 3:2) and seems unclear (at best) about the new birth. He reappears in chapter 7 and expresses a gentle voice of dissent against his fellow Jewish leaders. Something is surely happening in Nicodemus's life at this point, but it's unclear exactly what. He steps back on stage in chapter 19 to assist Joseph of Arimathea with spices to prepare Jesus' body for burial.

Nicodemus moves from darkness (John tells us three times that it was "at night" that he first came to Jesus) to the light of identification with a crucified Messiah. But John never tells us all we'd like to know. We see the wind blowing in Nicodemus's life. We hear its sound. While we still have questions about where it comes from and where it's going, we have no doubt of its reality.

I take encouragement from this narrative. Perhaps God is at work in our relatives' lives even when it appears that nothing is happening. This shouldn't cause us to sit back and do nothing. But it can help us trust that more is going on than just what we see. In the meantime, we can devote ourselves to prayer, step on the clutch before shifting gears, and ask God to help us find the right blend of boldness, sensitivity, and grace.

C. S. Lewis's perspective on time might help us along the way. If you're not familiar with his book, *The Screwtape Letters,* you should know it's a series of fictitious letters between one demon and another. The senior demon writes to train a novice about how to mess up a human. Hence, everything the writer puts forth as bad is really good and vice versa. The "Enemy" he speaks about is God. He writes:

The humans live in time but our Enemy destines them to eternity. He therefore, I believe, wants them to attend chiefly to two things, to eternity itself, and to that point of time which they call the Present. For the Present is the point at which time touches eternity. Of the present moment, and of it only, humans have an experience analogous to the experience which our Enemy has of reality as a whole; in it alone freedom and actuality are offered them. He would therefore have them continually concerned either with eternity (which means being concerned with Him) or with the Present—either meditating on their eternal union with, or separation from, Himself, or else obeying the present voice of conscience, bearing the present cross, receiving the present grace, giving thanks for the present pleasure.[5]

We live in time but are destined for eternity. We interact with family over dinner tables, while watching television, at vacation spots, making ordinary plans, discussing calendars, swapping recipes, and getting immersed in a host of other mundane activities that seem disconnected from eternity. But, in fact, they "touch eternity." So let us remember that all our interactions with family occur at that crucial intersection between the temporal and the eternal. We strive to love our relatives right where they're at for exactly who they are at this moment in time. We point them to eternity through the lens of the here and now. We enjoy life with them now and tell them of another life to come. We pray for them to come to faith sooner rather than later and ask God to grant us peace and joy regardless of his timetable.

Steps to Take

1. For which relatives have you been "waiting" the longest? Have you given up hope? Ask God to renew your heart. Have you grown weary? Ask God to remind you of his work in your life over the years.

---

[5] C. S. Lewis, *The Screwtape Letters* (San Francisco: HarperCollins, 2001), 75–76.

Have you grown impatient and said things you regret? Go ask for forgiveness. In other words, take stock of your long-term relationships and ask God to guide your next steps. There are times to just stay the course, and there are other times to make strategic turns. Ask God for guidance and guts.

2. Relationships with siblings pose a unique challenge. They may be the ones with whom we'll have the longest relationships. The problem of assumed but unexpressed love may be most pervasive between siblings. If this is true in your situation, find ways to express the words that have gone unspoken for too long—perhaps with the next birthday card or Christmas present. Breaking the silence can open pathways for the deepest conversations you've ever had.

3. If you came to faith out of another major world religion (Judaism, Islam, Buddhism, etc.), you'll need to do some research about the best methods of witnessing to that specific worldview. You may think that because you came out of that faith, you already know how to evangelize into it. But sometimes close proximity blurs our vision. It is wise to take advice from missionaries who interact with that world on a daily basis. For example, Jews for Jesus and Chosen People Ministries can give you great insight and provide proven resources for the task of reaching Jewish families. People who work with Muslims recommend Answering Islam at www.answering-islam .org (be careful not to type *.com*). Similar resources exist for Mormonism, Jehovah's Witness, a variety of cults, and other religions. It would be worth the investment of time to study carefully the wealth of materials others have developed. Don't reinvent the wheel.

4. Certain cultures pose specific dynamic tensions that require particular attention as we take the long-term approach to witnessing. One helpful resource for Asian Christians is *Following Jesus without Dishonoring Your Parents: Asian American Discipleship.*[6] Wisdom from similar resources for other cultures are worth seeking out.

5. Give thanks for exactly where your relatives are right now. Find common-ground issues to enjoy together at this point in time—travel, music, sports, movies, books, history, etc. In most cases, they're going to be in your life for a long time. It would be nice for them to know you're interested in something besides Jesus.

---

[6] Jeanette Yep, Peter Cha, Susan Cho Van Riesen, Greg Jao, and Paul Tokunaga, *Following Jesus without Dishonoring Your Parents: Asian American Discipleship* (Downers Grove, IL: InterVarsity Press, 1998).

7

ETERNITY

Comforting and Yet Terrifying

As I began work on this chapter, my wife received an e-mail from her brother informing her that their father had just taken a turn for the worse. He had made several of these turns during the past year, but this one sounded real. The hospice nurse said it looked like he only had a few days left. Pam boarded an early morning flight the next day and arrived at her father's bedside in time to say good-bye. The next night he died. Meanwhile, Pam's mother entered the hospital with difficulty breathing. We all thought it was due to the stress of watching her husband of over fifty years leave this earth. But in fact, she had pneumonia, which was causing severe aggravation to her recently diagnosed pulmonary fibrosis.

Horrifically, the hospital staff determined she only had a few days left. Less than one week later, we held a dual memorial service. We all felt shell-shocked by the reality of death.

People face death in one of at least four different ways:

- They fear it with horror.
- They ignore it in denial.

- They cling to false hope through naïve universalist faith.
- They overcome it in the gospel.

Put another way, they say to death one of four statements:

- "Get away from me!"
- "I don't even think about you."
- "Death is just a natural part of life."
- "Death, where is your victory, where is your sting?"

Our task in evangelism centers on contrasting the first three responses to the fourth. The distinct nature of the finished work of the gospel delivers people from fear, denial, or false hope. When we point people to Christ, we show them a way that takes the sting out of death, thus making it something to anticipate instead of dread. As Dietrich Bonheoffer once preached, "Death is grace, the greatest gift of grace that God gives to people who believe in him."[1]

If we look further into that nighttime conversation between Jesus and Nicodemus in John 3, we see remarkable clarity that often escapes current discussions about death. Jesus could not have painted a more stark contrast when he declared, "For God so loved the world, that he gave his only Son, that whoever believes in him should not perish but have eternal life. For God did not send his Son into the world to condemn the world, but in order that the world might be saved through him. Whoever believes in him is not condemned, but whoever does not believe is condemned already, because he has not believed in the name of the only Son of God" (John 3:16–18).

---

[1] Quoted in Eric Metaxas, *Bonhoeffer: Pastor, Martyr, Prophet, Spy* (Nashville: Thomas Nelson, 2010), 531.

I'm sure you've heard or read many things about this passage, so allow me to point out just two components that relate to the task of evangelism.

First, there's good reason why people like to quote verse 16 without including verses 17 and 18. If you read it on its own, you might get away with overlooking the word "perish" and just zoom in on how much God loves you. No wonder this Scripture reference appears so ubiquitously. But the contrast between having "eternal life" and "perishing" gets lost in this abridgment. The wonder of Jesus' words to Nicodemus is that God would rescue anyone! We are all "condemned already"—for good reason. We have "not believed in the name of the only Son of God." In contrast to the American justice system where we are all presumed innocent until proven guilty, in God's courtroom, we are all presumed "condemned" (a word Jesus repeats three times) unless miraculously saved.

You'll find this truth noticeably absent at funerals and in the text of most sympathy cards. Quite often those cards and the notes people write in them assume people are "better off" now that they're no longer alive. That can only be said for those who have been delivered out of the domain of darkness. That's why the Bible calls them "saved."

Second, it's important not to skip the words "for" and "so" in verse 16. They allude back to the previous paragraph. There, Jesus compared his salvation to that of God's rescuing of the Israelites when they looked to the serpent on a pole. Do you remember that strange story back in Numbers 21? The people "spoke against God and against Moses . . ." (Num. 21:5), so God sent judgment upon them in the form of poisonous snakes. But he also provided a way of salvation. If the people would look upon a bronze serpent Moses crafted for this very purpose, the people would be spared the sentence of death. Do you see the parallel? In order for the wilderness whiners to get set free, they needed to turn from their self-righteous complaining to the saving hand of God. They needed to repent of their sin and trust in God as Savior. When we turn to Jesus, we need the same attitude of contrition.

That's why verse 16 begins with "for." It links together the two episodes of God's salvation. And the insertion of the word "so" makes the connection even more pronounced. Our first inclination is to think that Jesus said, "God *so* loved the world" to express *how much* love was involved. We see it as a quantitative statement. But it's really a qualitative statement, expressing the variety (rather than the volume) of God's love. It's a saving kind of love. It's also an undeserved kind of love. It's a love that provides atonement. God was perfectly just in sending the snakes in the wilderness and is equally just in allowing people to perish today. The marvel is that this same God who punishes sin also offers salvation.

And don't miss the use of the word "world." When John spoke of the world, he emphasized how wicked or fleeting or spiritually dangerous it was. D. A. Carson observes, "God's love is to be admired not because the world is so big and includes so many people, but because the world is so bad."[2]

This clear teaching of Jesus cuts two ways. It prompts joy for us as believers because we can have assurance of salvation. If a parent or grandparent or anyone we know dies "in the Lord" we grieve, but not "as others do who have no hope" (see 1 Thess. 4:13). Several people told me of the joy they found in knowing their parent was now with the Lord, even if they came to faith at the eleventh hour.

Paul told me of his seven-year running dialogue with his aging mother about faith. He called her on the phone *every day* on his way home from work. It just became part of his

---

[2] D. A. Carson, *The Gospel according to John* (Grand Rapids, MI: InterVarsity Press, 1991), 205.

daily commute. Before pulling out of the company parking lot, he read Scripture to his mother and then discussed it as he battled traffic. Even though she had never gone to church her entire life, as death loomed large, she began to open up to the gospel. When Paul became a believer in his mid-forties, he immediately shared his conversion story with his mother, and she (perhaps just to maintain closeness with her son, perhaps out of loneliness after her husband died, or perhaps just out of boredom) delighted in the daily elaborations on his basic testimony.

"Sometimes I just told my mother how life looked through a different set of lenses. The more ordinary the situation, the more she seemed to pay attention. I kept thinking it would be the dramatic stories of emotional highs I experienced in a worship service, but she asked the most questions when I told her that my newfound faith helped me forgive my wife for some tiny offense."

He emphasized to me how the regular routine of the phone calls enhanced the conversations. I asked him if he ran out of things to talk about. "Didn't the frequency of the calls make it harder to find topics to address?" I wondered. "No. It's just the opposite," he told me. "The less often you talk on the phone, the less there is to talk about. Talking every day made it easier to build one long continuing narrative." Of course, throughout those seven years Paul made numerous trips so he could talk face to face. On one of the final visits, he simply asked his mother if she was ready to place her trust in Christ the same way he had done years before. It all made sense to her now, and she said yes. He prayed a prayer, phrase by phrase, and asked her to repeat it, phrase by phrase. Less than a year later, she went to be with the Savior she had just recently met.

"People tell me they're amazed at how much time I spent on the phone with my mother, but I don't regret a minute of it," he smiled. "Knowing she's with the Lord now makes it all seem worthwhile."

But what about the pain from knowing, with a good amount of certainty, that a departed loved one is not with the Lord? How do we overcome that sorrow? That's the second way John 3:16 cuts.

Dallas told me he can only remember crying two times in his life—when he learned of his father's diagnosis of a brain tumor and when he stood at the funeral grappling with the reality that his father never responded to the gospel. An atheist, his dad refused to pray for healing when friends offered, saying, "Why should I waste my time?" For the first eighteen years of his life, Dallas followed in his father's skeptical footsteps. But in his freshman year of college, he met a group of Christians who had a joy he wanted. Being the logical type, he read the New Testament straight through and posed many tough questions to his classmates. Somewhere during the spring semester of his freshman year, he embraced the faith—just in time to watch his father's rapid decline in health.

"Of course, I wish my father was in heaven, but I have absolutely no reason to think he is. I have to accept the truth of the Bible as a more reliable source of truth than what I want to be true." He said these words with a tremendous amount of pain in his voice. I thought, at any moment, I would witness the third episode of tears in his life. In fact, I hoped I would. The tears would have helped his grieving process.

He continued, "I have prayed many times, 'Jesus, help me to see things the way you see them.' That has helped me a lot. I've come to realize that Christ is greater than my dad. I mean, I loved my dad, but he wasn't perfect. In fact, there are some things about him that bring a lot of shame. So I have a choice. I can renounce Christ and choose my dad as the greatest person in my life. Or I can renounce my dad, in the sense that I won't look to him to be the greatest person in my life, and choose Christ as the One I look to. Even though it's painful, when I look at the choice that clearly, it's an easy decision."

This young man showed a tremendous amount of wisdom for his age. Others much older have echoed his sentiments with statements like, "I have to look to God, not to my family, as my hope. That's true for when they're alive and after they're gone."

I can only add that there must be far more to the title "the God of all comfort" (2 Cor. 1:3) than we usually consider. "All" must really mean all. We wonder how we can ever find joy after losing an unsaved loved one. But many people have. Just as we wonder how some people can find hope and joy in the midst of excruciating physical pain, somehow they do. In fact, I find it is more common that people affirm their faith in the midst of pain than abandon it. The skeptics often point to others who suffer as their rationale for disbelief. But the people in the wheelchairs or the cancer units tell stories of the glorious Savior they're looking forward to seeing. In a parallel way, the God of *all* comfort, the God who promises a peace "which surpasses all understanding" (Phil. 4:7), can offer a balm to the soul when we lose someone who never bent the knee to the Savior.

Of course, many people just don't know where their departed relatives have gone. Their loved ones' relationship with Christ was never as clear as they would have liked. They proclaimed, gave books, left tracts, read Scripture, asked questions, and even sang songs in the ears of the dying, but they never got the affirmation of faith that would bring a confident assurance about their standing before God. What then?

David told me he wished he knew if his parents were in heaven. But he just doesn't. They spent a lot of time in a liberal church that preached a great deal about social involvement

187

and moralistic self-help. But the term "born again" never came from the pulpit. After David came to saving faith through a Christian businessmen's organization, he shared the gospel with his parents, and they both responded positively.

But that was over thirty years ago, and David saw only sporadic evidence of a gospel-changed life before they died not too long ago. Over the years, his parents quoted from the Bible on numerous occasions. But they drew equally upon the Dalai Lama, Mark Twain, and Gandhi. And that was *before* the dementia kicked in. Who knows what they really believed or understood?

"I finally gave up trying to figure it all out," David told me. "In fact, I felt liberated when I realized that my demand to know of their salvation was really a kind of idolatry. I confessed it as sin and began to see God cleanse me from such pride. Now I trust that God is a gracious God and he knows things far better than I do. God can sort out my parents' theology and see their hearts. I hope I'll see my parents in heaven. If I were a betting man . . . well, I'm not a betting man, and even if I were, betting about someone else's salvation sounds like a bad idea. For now, I choose to emphasize the good memories and accept my limitations."

As frustrating as that may sound, I believe David displays great wisdom.

Phil, a pastor for many years, also shared with me some insight he tells members of his congregation when they lose relatives who didn't know Jesus. As difficult as it may be to comprehend now, when we stand face to face in God's presence, the glory and beauty of the Lord must be so overwhelming that it wipes away every tear—including the ones we've shed for family. If we can grant that heaven will be far better than we could ever imagine, we can accept that, somehow, God can do what we currently think is impossible.

Quite a few people told me of the great frustration of having so-called Christian relatives who showed no sign of rebirth. "You're writing a book on how to witness to family?" one friend said. "Write a section on how to witness to *Christian* family!" I knew what he meant. There are many people who attend church services and church activities but seem to believe a form of bland humanistic self-help that gleans more wisdom from the likes of *Chicken Soup for the Soul* than from the Bible. It is worth considering that they might actually hold to a different religion than Christianity. Didn't Jesus warn of wolves in sheep's clothing (see Matt. 7:15)? And doesn't the New Testament warn of the need to discern truth from error—error in a form that sounds so very close to the truth (see the books of Colossians and Hebrews)?

At the beginning of the twentieth century, theologian J. Gresham Machen keenly observed that "despite the liberal use of traditional phraseology, modern liberalism not only is a different religion from Christianity but belongs in a totally different class of religions."[3] His words are no less true today. In fact, current disturbing trends seem reminiscent of that old 1920s liberalism. So it is quite possible that relatives and close friends fill their Sunday morning schedules the same way you do—by going to church. But what they hear and what they believe may be light-years from the message of the cross.

In these cases, the task of "witnessing to Christians" is the opposite of "finding common ground." It's exactly the common ground that has obscured the gospel. You quote Bible verses. They quote them too. You talk about God's love, grace, and forgiveness, and they nod their heads in agreement. But you're thinking of vastly different realities. What you need to do is distinguish the gospel from popular imposters. It is best to do this in a general way, rather than pointing the

---

[3] J. Gresham Machen, *Christianity and Liberalism* (New York: Macmillan, 1923), 7.

finger at "what your church teaches verses what my church teaches." Instead, conversations need to go along the lines of "here's what's so different about the gospel. Here's how the gospel is different from religion."[4]

And just to make things a bit muddier, there is a possibility that some people may come to faith in the final days of their lives, even if we never hear them say so. I realize I am treading on thin ice when I say this but it does seem possible to me that if people have heard the gospel sometime in their lives, they could respond during their final days of consciousness with the inevitable reality of death right around the corner.

Neuroscience, the study of the brain, may be the most rapidly developing field of inquiry today. It is amazing what we are finding out about how the brain works during sleep, while listening to music, and even while people say "the long good-bye" through Alzheimer's disease. Someday we may also learn what people think, believe, and see as they die. Is it at least possible that some people who never showed signs of belief while they were "with it" could cast themselves upon the mercy of Christ once they became silenced by dementia, Alzheimer's, brain tumors, or senility? I'm willing to hold that out as a possibility. I am certainly not offering that as an encouragement to hold back and withhold a bold pronouncement of the gospel. In fact, I'm offering it as an endorsement of bold proclamation while you can—share the good news with confidence that God's Word is a two-edged sword that can cut through "the division of soul and of spirit, of joints and of marrow" (Heb. 4:12)—maybe even the ravages of fatal diseases.

Implications for Evangelism
Pressing Urgency
First, the reality of eternity bids us to evangelize boldly. Let's state the obvious. Evangelism entails a significant amount of

---

[4] Some of the clearest distinctions between the gospel and religion are found in Timothy Keller's *The Prodigal God* (New York: Dutton, 2008).

urgency. Everyone dies and faces judgment. Some will find refuge in the atonement purchased by the blood of Christ. Others will rely on their own merits, which cannot save them. They will perish. Therefore, our message carries the freight of a warning.

After all the pre-evangelism, the silent displays of love, the waiting, the compassion, the empathy, the seeking common ground, the stepping on the clutch before shifting gears, and all the rest, we still need to sound the alarm of impending judgment by a righteous God. This urgency never wanes. For aging parents or grandparents, the reality of the end of this earthly life looms right around the corner. But even for younger relatives, the dangers of this world (automobile accidents, increasing violence, natural disasters, etc.) all bring frequent reminders of the uncertainty of the future.

Some people think quickly on their feet and can come up with just the right words without rehearsal. Most cannot. So don't count on your quick wit or spontaneous eloquence for crucial conversations. Practice what you need to say regarding death and eternal life. Write it out if that helps. And don't wait for it to feel comfortable. Say the uncomfortable before it's too late.

You might need to precede your evangelistic presentation with statements like this:

"Grandpa, I know you've told me you don't like to talk about religion. But I need to tell you that I'm concerned about you. Can you please listen to something I want to say about going to heaven?"

"Mom, we've never really talked about what happens after you die. I know this is uncomfortable, but nothing could be more important."

"Aunt Edna, you've always been so kind to me but we've never spoken about something that's really crucial for you right now. Can I please tell you about the most important thing in my life?"

If your relative is a reader, there are some good pointed books that boldly address the reality of death and God's offer of salvation. Billy Graham's *Death and the Life After* or Erwin Lutzer's *How You Can Be Sure That You Will Spend Eternity with God* are just two of many helpful tools for those more open when they have pain as a constant companion.[5]

You may have heard the statistic that 85 percent of all the people who ever accept Christ do so before they turn eighteen. I have never seen documentation for that stat. Even if it was true at one point in time, I'm not convinced it still is. Just as our culture shifts, so do evangelistic trends. Even if that figure is accurate, the remaining 15 percent still make up a sizeable amount of people. That statistic must not discourage us from witnessing to older people. God is more powerful than the aging process.

As I told people about my writing of this book, I was amazed how many people voluntarily shared stories of parents and grandparents in their seventies and eighties coming to faith. Not surprisingly, some people think about death when they get that old! Bob led his eighty-seven-year-old uncle to saving faith after Uncle Ernie shared, "Bobby, I'm afraid to die."

Lois told me she finally changed her tactic in witnessing to her father after thirty-five years of giving him Bibles, books, and tracts. She came to faith as a teen through a church's youth ministry, but her parents never went to church. In their old age they simply withdrew into a shell of fear and reclusiveness. Nothing worked. Her mother's painful death left her father even more depressed and paranoid. So she started pleading with the Lord to bring other Christians into his life who would witness to him as peers.

And that's exactly what God did. In his retirement village, a fishing club started up, and four guys came knocking on

---

[5] Billy Graham, *Death and the Life After* (Waco, TX: Word, 1987); Erwin Lutzer, *How You Can Be Sure That You Will Spend Eternity with God* (Chicago: Moody, 1996).

his door to see if he'd like to join them. "No!" he grouchily told them. But they wouldn't give up. And eventually, Lois's Dad went fishing. Apparently these guys saw themselves as fishers of another kind because they started inviting him to church as well. On Easter Sunday, Lois's father called her and said, "I never knew Jesus rose from the dead! Why didn't you tell me?"

Lois just laughed all the way through her recounting of the story of her father's conversion. "I must have told him fifty times about the resurrection. He just never had ears to hear. Now he's a totally different person. He's not afraid to go out. He drives everywhere by himself. In fact, last week he drove over a thousand miles to see my sister. And the first thing he packed was his Bible."

Clear Consciences

Second, the reality of eternity requires us to evangelize freely. We need to be careful not to take on responsibility for others' responses. Too many people told me they felt culpable for their family's lack of response to the gospel. They racked themselves with guilt because they hadn't done enough to convert their relatives. Some even appealed to Scripture for this shame. They told me their pastor preached regularly that Ezekiel taught we are all watchmen, and if we don't warn people about hell, "their blood will be on our hands." (They point to Ezek. 3:16–19 and 33:1–6 for this rationale.)

This is surely an odd way to read the Bible. It chooses certain passages to foist an agenda upon readers without taking into account immediate context or the overall flow of Scripture's story line. When people apply God's commission to Ezekiel to themselves, I often wonder why they don't also take on all the other commands God gave that prophet. Shouldn't they also eat scrolls (Ezek. 3:1), draw on clay tablets (4:1), lie on their left side for 390 days, their right side for forty days, and eat strange foods (4:4–13)? The list could go on, in some very odd directions. If ever there were a unique calling upon a one-of-a-kind prophet, Ezekiel fits the bill. One wonders what kind of applications would come out of their reading of Hosea!

This kind of selective application often gets people into trouble. It produces a guilt that flies in the faith of new covenant blessings such as, "There is therefore now no condemnation for those who are in Christ Jesus" (Rom. 8:1). The whole notion of one person being held "accountable" for someone else's blood contradicts the accomplishment of the cross, the new covenant emphasis upon individual faith (see Jer. 31:27–30), and the difference between an old covenant prophet and a new covenant saint.

To add further complications, this guilt-induced evangelism rarely works. People who tell their relatives about Christ because they want to get out from under a yoke of guilt distort the message. Their motivation stems from a concern for their own welfare ("I've got to make sure I won't be held accountable for your blood") more than the soul of their unsaved relative. People can tell when you're set free by your religion and when you're oppressed by it. They'll be attracted to the former. They'll want nothing to do with the latter.

Theological Tensions
Third, the reality of eternity urges us to evangelize even without total theological understanding of the whole process. I found it odd that several people told me of hesitancy to witness (to anyone, not just to family) because of theological confusion. Randall told me he was "stuck" at the point of trying to figure out how evangelism works if God is sovereign. "If God predestines people, why do I even need to witness?" he asked. "Because that's the system God designed," I told him. "But I don't understand how that fits together. God

chooses but he also holds people responsible. And he wants us to get involved in the process. I can't put all the pieces together," he trailed off.

"Maybe you don't need to," I responded. When he wrinkled his brow in confusion, I elaborated. "Maybe figuring it all out isn't a prerequisite for evangelism. At least, I hope it isn't, or no one will ever share the gospel. I think it might be beyond human ability to comprehend. I don't think that should hold us back. In fact, I think it can liberate us."

The rest of my conversation with Randall centered on Paul's words at the end of Romans 11. After three whole chapters of pondering the intersection of God's sovereignty and people's responsibility, Paul concluded, "Oh, the depth of the riches and wisdom and knowledge of God! How unsearchable are his judgments and how inscrutable his ways!" (Rom. 11:33). If Paul couldn't totally figure it out, what makes us think we will? If certain things are "unsearchable" and "inscrutable," shouldn't we be suspicious of explanations that seem totally understandable or easily fathomable?

J. I. Packer's classic work, *Evangelism and the Sovereignty of God* turns the whole question on its head and liberates us to evangelize with confidence. He writes, "Some fear that belief in the sovereign grace of God leads to the conclusion that evangelism is pointless, since God will save His elect anyway, whether they hear the gospel or not. This, as we have seen, is a false conclusion based on a false assumption. But now we must go further, and point out that the truth is just the opposite. So far from making evangelism pointless, the sovereignty of God in grace is the one thing that prevents evangelism from being pointless. For it creates the possibility—indeed, the certainty—that evangelism will be fruitful. Apart from it, there is not even a possibility of evangelism being fruitful."[6]

Don't let theological confusion stymie your efforts to share the good news. I'm not encouraging intellectual laziness when I say this. Diligent study of the Scriptures and theology provide a deep reservoir from which to nourish your own soul and reach out with a fuller message. But realize that some levels of understanding lie outside the realm of human capabilities.

Difficult Conversations

Fourth, the reality of eternity presses us to evangelize even through discomfort. Not all families produce the dynamics for completely happy endings. For some people, anger still permeates in painful ways. And, contrary to the silly cliché, time does not heal all wounds. As people approach death, the need for resolution should not be ignored.

Communication scholars Maureen Keeley and Julie Yingling have written a helpful guide aptly titled *Final Conversations*. They suggest that final conversations can confirm relationships, provide closure, prepare people for impending loss, and resolve pain so as to bring peace after a loved one dies. They comment, "Coping with challenging tasks is easier if we've done them before, but few of us are eager to practice dealing with death. In our culture death means dealing with the unknown while in the throes of extreme emotional distress and challenging conditions. . . .What amazed us is that, when asked, almost everyone wants an opportunity to talk with the dying at least one more time before it is too late."[7]

---

[6] J. I. Packer, *Evangelism and the Sovereignty of God* (Chicago: InterVarsity Press, 1961), 106. This very helpful book is essential reading for anyone who wants to share the gospel with freedom and boldness.

[7] Maureen P. Keeley and Julie M. Yingling, *Final Conversations: Helping the Living and the Dying Talk to Each Other* (Acton, MA: VanderWyk & Burnham, 2007), 5. As far as I can tell, the authors do not take a specific religious stance, Christian or otherwise.

Here's what Keeley and Yingling don't say: Christians, if they avail themselves to the firm standing they have in Christ, have an advantage in facing the death of a loved one. We don't deny death, because we saw it conquered by the resurrection. We don't fear death, because we were purchased by the blood of Christ. Even when talking to an unsaved relative, we don't shy away from the uncomfortable, because Christ's comfort overcomes all difficulties. We can dare to bring up the topics others avoid. We can proclaim a certain message when everyone else is mouthing vague platitudes or "lite" clichés. We can handle rejection because we've been accepted. We can also choose to forgive dying relatives even if it's totally unmerited, because that's exactly the kind of forgiveness we received from Christ.

Pieter can make just about anyone's hair stand on end with the horrible stories of his childhood. The number of divorces, the level of alcoholism, and the frequency of physical abuse could make even the worst reality show look like a child's cartoon. When he came to faith during college, he found a new family that joyfully replaced the sick one back at home. He spent vacations and holidays with newfound Christian brothers and sisters because he never wanted to be with his family ever again, especially at holiday time, when the booze flowed freely. He signed up for every summer mission trip possible just to stay far away from home.

After graduation, he joined the staff of his church and ministered to young adults. He brought comfort to many and offered a message of grace, regardless of how bad a person's background.

But then his father summoned him to his deathbed. That's an overstatement, but not by much. Pieter went to visit his father when it appeared the end was near. They had made somewhat of a restoration of their relationship when Pieter

---

But Christians can benefit greatly from their wisdom after interviewing dozens of people who have had meaningful conversations with dying relatives.

unilaterally forgave his father years before. Now, his father wanted to talk, knowing he had less than a month to live.

"I was a good father, wasn't I?" were the words Pieter said his dad used.

"What was I supposed to say?" Pieter exclaimed to me as we talked at a church picnic not too long ago.

"I don't know. What did you say?" I asked.

"Well, I'll tell you what I wanted to say. I wanted to say, 'No! You weren't a good father. You were a drunk, an abuser, an adulterer, a cheater, a jerk.'"

"But you didn't say that, did you?" I smiled. And he smiled, too.

"No. I did pause for a while, though. I wanted to get this right. I told him, 'Dad, I think you did as good a job as you could do. But you know what, nobody does all that they should. We all blow it at some point or another."

Pieter paused and swallowed deeply and then went on.

"My father had never responded to anything I had ever told him about the Lord or about my coming to faith or anything spiritual. But now he was listening to me so I shared the gospel with him. It was like I hit the 'play' button on a recorder where I had stored a gospel presentation I had said hundreds of times to others. I went into automatic pilot and told him the whole story of Jesus dying on the cross for his sins. I needed to do it that way—kind of like a robot— because if I thought about all the emotions regarding my father, I would have stopped too many times to insert my anger."

"How did he respond?"

"He trusted Christ! Three weeks before he died. It was amazing. And confusing. And upsetting."

"Why was it upsetting?" I asked.

"Why didn't he do this earlier? Why couldn't we have had some time together in a good father-son relationship?

Anyway, I'll see him in heaven. We'll have lots of good times there."

I applauded Pieter for choosing a gospel route with his father rather than a revengeful one. Sure, he could have answered his father's question differently. Perhaps some schools of counseling would have encouraged him to do so. But the gospel of grace brings resolution and peace and love. Pieter talks about his father now with peaceful forgiveness and joy. He would never have found that without first venturing into some uncomfortable territory.

Stark Clarity
Fifth, the reality of eternity forces us to evangelize with clear declarations. A short recap of some church history will help set what I'm about to say into a larger context.

At crucial moments in history, the church has faced various crises of belief. How we responded to challenges to core tenets of the faith shaped the people of God and distinguished orthodoxy from heresy. During the first centuries, the age of the church fathers, the crisis was about the doctrine of Christ. Some people questioned his dual nature, saying he couldn't be both God and man. But the church responded with documents like the Apostles' Creed and the Nicene Creed and affirmed that indeed Jesus was fully God and fully man.

During the Reformation, the crisis was about the doctrine of salvation. Some people questioned whether salvation was by faith. But the church responded with a series of statements using the key word "alone." We are saved by grace alone, through faith alone, by Christ alone.

At the beginning of the twentieth century, we faced another crisis, one about the nature of the Scriptures. Some people questioned whether they were authoritative and historically reliable. In tragic ways, churches and entire denominations split over the Bible, during what has been called "the fundamentalist-modernist" conflict. The fundamentalists responded with clear affirmations that God has spoken and the Bible is indeed his Word. To apply the wording of one of Francis Schaeffer's book titles, we affirmed that "he is there and he is not silent."

Today, at a time some historians identify as a shift from modernism to postmodernism, we face another crisis—one of knowing. Now the question is not just whether the Bible is God's authoritative Word but whether we can know *anything* from *any* source. Some people throw their hands in the air and say, "Who knows anything anyway?" Disturbingly, some who call themselves evangelicals acquiesce, unwittingly undermining their ability to say anything with confidence or clarity.

To be sure, God has not revealed everything we'd like to know. Moses preached, "The secret things belong to the LORD our God," but then he immediately added, "but the things that are revealed belong to us and to our children forever, that we may do all the words of this law" (Deut. 29:29). Do you see the confidence this can instill?

No wonder the apostle John began his first epistle with these bold affirmations, "That which we have seen and heard we proclaim also to you . . ." (1 John 1:3), and with equal boldness, he concluded his epistle with, "And this is the testimony, that God gave us eternal life, and this life is in his Son. Whoever has the Son has life; whoever does not have the Son of God does not have life. I write these things to you who believe in the name of the Son of God that you may know that you have eternal life" (1 John 5:11–13).

Do you hear the clarity? Can you feel the confidence?

Victor certainly did as he read those verses to his father just one day before his father's death. Even though Victor was a very young Christian, he had been instructed about the crucial issue of assurance of salvation. Together with the guys in his campus Bible study, he had memorized 1 John

5:11–13. Now he sensed these same words could clarify the gospel to his father, who knew he had only hours to live. A lifelong doubter who only occasionally attended church merely for the cultural experience, he listened to his son with more careful attention than he had listened to any sermon.

Even though his words were unpolished, Victor spoke softly by his father's hospital bedside and said, "Dad, this verse says you only go to heaven if you have the Son. That means you have to tell God you want to trust in what Jesus did on the cross to pay for your sins. You have to tell God you're sorry for trying to run your own life without his help. You have to tell him you're sorry for your sins—all the things that God would not want you to do. Do you believe this?"

By this point, the combination of the disease and the pain medications made communication practically impossible. His father merely stared at Victor with a look that seemed to say, "I want to."

To this day, Victor shrugs his shoulders and wonders what his father understood and what he told God in his final hours.

"But it's not for lack of clarity," he explains. "I'm confident that God's Word is clear and it can cut through anything—even morphine."

You were probably hoping for a happier ending to that story. I heard too many testimonies of "I'm not sure where my parents are" to only present happy endings. Other people did indeed tell me of deathbed conversions, aided by the reading of Scripture. Despite theological debates around them, some passages state things far more clearly to people who are dying than we can ever imagine. Readings of Scripture beside hospice beds may be some of the most fruitful evangelistic campaigns in the history of the church.

Singer-songwriter Sally Klein O'Connor tells two stories, one happy, one sad.[8] Raised in a Jewish home, she only heard Jesus' name used as a swear word. But after college, she came to know Jesus as Lord, and he made her a new creation. "Still, I had a very hard relationship with my father. All we had was anger between us. When I was a young believer in my twenties, my father and I fought *every* time we got together. My parents had split up, and whenever I saw my father, I did not see a person, I only saw a list of all the wrongs he had done—to me and to my mom and to others."

One morning, when the potential for another fight started building, Sally dismissed herself from her father's presence and went to her room to cool off. It was there, she says, that God showed her *she* needed to change. The pattern of fighting wasn't helping anyone.

"I have no other way to describe it other than to say it was an instantaneous healing. I wish all my prayers were answered that way, but they're not. But this one was a total healing."

She went back and told her father she loved him. She thinks that might have been the first time she ever said those words to him. And she's quite certain it was the first time she heard him say, "I love you, too."

"For the next two years, my Dad couldn't do anything to offend me. You can't imagine how dramatic a change that was. I came to a place of forgiveness and it all happened in a day." That began a long series (more than nine years) of conversations about the Lord. He acknowledged that their newfound friendship only existed because of Sally's faith.

---

[8] Unlike other names used in this book, this is a real name. Sally, along with her husband Michael, have a beautiful ministry of healing and joy through music and literature. You can hear more of their story at Improbable People, www.improbable people.org.

As his health began to weaken, Sally became his primary caretaker. The dramatic change in Sally's heart toward her father prompted her to remark to her husband Michael, "I don't want to sit at the banquet table of the lamb without him there." That was all the image Michael needed to pen these words, which Sally later set to music:

So here we are again, another Sunday dinner
I bought the best rosé that I could find
But the silence, like the bottle, breathes between us
We both know I've got much more on my mind

You'd rather sit and talk to me about the weather
And how the soaps have lately got you down
But when I start to talk about forever
I know you're getting picture without sound

I just want to see you there
Please don't ask me not to care
I don't want to sit at his table
Next to an empty chair
I just really want to see you there

I know that you don't really think I'm blind or crazy
Though sometimes I believe that I must be
What kind of lunatic throws out all reason
And gives her life to someone she can't see

I wish I had more faith so I could just let go
Or short of that composure to pretend
But I think the time is short and, yes, I'm scared
I need to know we'll meet again

I just want to see you there
Please don't ask me not to care
I don't want to sit at his table
Next to an empty chair
I just really want to see you there

So in a quiet moment
Won't you ask Him if He's real
Then reach out and touch His face

I just want to see you there
Please don't ask me not to care
I don't want to sit at his table
Next to an empty chair
I just really want to see you there[9]

As Sally began to sing this song at the close of all her con-
certs, the Lord impressed upon Michael to offer copies of this
song for free. "It was as if the Lord told me, 'You're not to
make a dime off this song.' So we started giving away copies
of cassette tapes (Yes, it was that long ago!) and then CDs, but
Sally always told her audience, 'The recordings are free but
they're not without charge.'"

The charge, Michael explains, was to take this record-
ing and give it to an unsaved friend or relative as a bridge
to share the gospel with them. The song isn't the gospel, but
given the tenderness of the lyrics and the power of music, it
could open hearts in profound ways.

Over the next twenty years, they gave away over twenty-
five thousand copies of the song and, ever increasingly, they
started to hear story after story after story of relatives who
had come to faith in the Messiah.

If ever you would have guessed which of Sally's parents
would come to faith, it would have been her mother. Sally
and her mother were very close. She was intelligent and cor-
dial and always willing to discuss deep issues—but she hated
religion. Sally's father was quite different.

When Sally's father's health required more consistent care,
she sensed the Lord telling her to "wash his feet," and in

---

[9] "I Just Want to See You There," words and music by Michael and Sally O'Connor © Copyright 1991 Improbable People Ministries. Used by permission. All rights reserved.

dozens of different ways that's exactly what she did. Michael and Sally's six-year-old daughter started praying for her grandfather every day.

Sally's sacrificial love broke through, and, five years before his death, he prayed with her to trust Jesus as Lord. (Immediately after saying, "Amen," he added, "My mother would kill me!") Those final five years brought transformation and gentleness. Even though he said he would never tell anyone about his faith in Jesus, he witnessed to relatives every chance he could and even wrote an extensive repentance letter to his wife.

By contrast, Sally's mother grew tougher rather than softer. Numerous times, she expressed anger that Sally "would be so cruel as to think that I'm going to hell." Nothing ever seemed to connect about the holiness of God, his judgment of sin, the whole point of atonement, or who Jesus was. Nothing.

Sally told me, "My mother couldn't talk for the last week of her life, so I don't know what was going on with her. I hope with all my heart that somewhere in her heart the Lord revealed himself to her and she received him as Lord, but I don't know. Only God knows."

Two dominant worldviews vie for our affections. One sees this life as all there is. The other sees this life as preparation for the next. One thinks only in terms of the temporal. The other values the temporal because it sees it in light of the eternal. The first way does all that it can to avoid thinking about death. The other faces death squarely. The first speaks only of people "living in our hearts" after they die. The other envisions "a great multitude that no one could number, from every nation, from all tribes and peoples and languages, standing before the throne and before the Lamb, clothed in white robes, with palm branches in their hands, and crying out with a loud voice, 'Salvation belongs to our God who sits on the throne, and to the Lamb!'" (Rev. 7:9–10).

What we say and do in this life can make an eternal difference in the next one.

Steps to Take

1. Meditate on Scripture passages that describe heaven. Allow the images to encourage and strengthen your convictions about the afterlife. Read books that unapologetically and uncompromisingly discuss heaven. One of my favorites is Joni Eareckson Tada's *Heaven: Your Real Home*.[10]

2. If you haven't already started doing so, start praying for God to bring other people into the lives of your relatives who will proclaim the gospel. Sometimes peers can say the exact same words you've said dozens of times, but they might be able to get through. Swallow the pride that thinks witnessing to your loved ones all depends on you and that no one else can introduce your relatives to the Lord.

3. If you had only ten minutes to lead someone to salvation on his deathbed, could you do it? What would you say? Prepare a message that progresses all the way to, "Would you like to tell God you want to trust in Jesus as your Savior?" If it helps to write down what you would say, take the time to do so. Include 1 John 5:11–13 or another Scripture that calls for a clear decision.

4. It may be helpful to do some reading about the dynamics of aging. You may think you already know all you need to, but the research about aging has unlocked many doors in recent years. One helpful

---

[10] Joni Eareckson Tada, *Heaven: Your Real Home* (Grand Rapids, MI: Zondervan, 2001).

resource is Mary Pipher's *Another Country*.[11] This beautiful book exudes grace and compassion for the elderly and can help you as you live out the book's subtitle, *Navigating the Emotional Terrain of Our Elders*.

5. Choose some materials (books, CDs, DVDs, etc.) that can serve as pre-evangelistic tools for aging relatives (such as Billy Graham's book or Michael and Sally Klein O'Connor's CD). Start building a collection of tools for when the time is right; it'll be here sooner than you think. You'll want to do the research and purchasing now before you're in crisis mode.

---

[11] Mary Pipher, *Another Country* (New York, NY: Riverhead Books, 1999).

EPILOGUE

The Jewish community collects stories that highlight their minority identity in a predominantly Gentile world. One memorable tale tells of a young boy who asked his rabbi, "What's the difference between Jews and other people?" The rabbi replied, "Oh, Jews are just like everyone else . . . only more so."

I often wonder if witnessing to family is just like witnessing to everyone else . . . only more so. Witnessing takes time. With family, it takes even more time. Witnessing involves the expression of love. With family, that love flows deeper but requires clearer expression. Witnessing encompasses a comprehensive worldview. With family, we have a wider range of common experiences in which to shine the glow of the gospel.

I keep this in mind when people ask me for a nutshell summary of my book. I offer the memorable slogan, "Witnessing to family takes TLC." I hope they catch my reference to "Tender, Loving Care" but then I tell them I mean something else. "T" stands for time, "L" stands for love, and "C" stands for comprehensiveness. These three were the common denominators I heard in the stories people told me. You need a longer-term perspective when it comes to family. You need a deeper reservoir of love. And you probably need to come in the side door by presenting the gospel as comprehensive in its effects, not just as a ticket into heaven.

But I hope you won't settle for a nutshell summary. Some topics are far more complex. That is certainly true of the expansive topic of the kingdom of God, of which evangelism is just a part. Jesus offered numerous illustrations and parables to help us grasp the kingdom's scope. On one occasion, he asked, "With what can we compare the kingdom of God, or what parable shall we use for it?" (Mark 4:30). He wanted his hearers to realize that no solitary image captures the complexity and enormity of the topic. Surely witnessing to family shares similar complex dynamics.

In Mark 4, Jesus tells three kingdom-illustrating parables that all talk about seed—how seed falls upon different kinds of soils, how some seed grows even without constant human attention, and how some seed has the potential to grow far beyond our imaginations. Some reflection upon these parables can help us sustain the long-term, loving, comprehensive perspective we need as we witness to family members, close friends, and others who know us well.

The first parable encourages us that even though some seed falls on ground that cannot produce a crop, other seed does:

> And he was teaching them many things in parables, and in his teaching he said to them: "Listen! A sower went out to sow. And as he sowed, some seed fell along the path, and the birds came and devoured it. Other seed fell on rocky ground, where it did not have much soil, and immediately it sprang up, since it had no depth of soil. And when the sun rose, it was scorched, and since it had no root, it withered away. Other seed fell among thorns, and the thorns grew up and choked it, and it yielded no grain. And other seeds fell into good soil and produced grain, growing up and increasing and yielding thirtyfold and sixtyfold and a hundredfold." And he said, "He who has ears to hear, let him hear." (Mark 4:2–9)

Fortunately for us, Jesus gave us the interpretation we need to understand this parable. When asked to explain it, he said,

> The sower sows the word. And these are the ones along the path, where the word is sown: when they hear, Satan

immediately comes and takes away the word that is sown in them. And these are the ones sown on rocky ground: the ones who, when they hear the word, immediately receive it with joy. And they have no root in themselves, but endure for a while; then, when tribulation or persecution arises on account of the word, immediately they fall away. And others are the ones sown among thorns. They are those who hear the word, but the cares of this world and the deceitfulness of riches and the desires for other things enter in and choke the word, and it proves unfruitful. But those that were sown on the good soil are the ones who heard the word and accept it and bear fruit, thirtyfold and sixtyfold and a hundredfold. (Mark 4:14–20)

Note that the sower sows the same seed on different soils. You can say the exact same words, gift wrap the exact same books, share the exact same tracts, and doodle the exact same diagram on a napkin, and one relative will not even give you the time of day while another asks you to elaborate.

Some of your relatives may be deceived by the Devil so it feels like your words are falling upon deaf ears. Spiritually speaking, they are. Some respond positively at first, but after time, with the realities of life's inevitable disappointments or pressures from skeptical outsiders, they show their true colors as ones who never really got it. Others show a similar positive response at first, but get sidelined by other things—not the negative ones, like trials or persecutions, but the positive ones, like prosperity, success, pleasure, and positive approval ratings from this world. It's amazing how long those drugs can seem to satisfy.

Ed must have wondered which soil represented his father. Even though Ed's mother was a godly woman who brought her son to church every Sunday, his dad stayed at home and smoked cigarettes, drank alcohol, and watched television. Ed shared two memories of what those Sundays were like: At church, he and his mother sat up in the balcony where they could hide due to the shame of not having the "man of the house" accompany them. (Such was the culture in parts of our country many years ago.) At home, his father was particularly grumpy on Sundays, more so than during the week.

When Ed was in high school, his mother died, prompting further depression and destructive behavior by his father. So when Ed got the chance to escape and move away to go to college, he did just that, rarely going back home to visit the father he didn't care for or respect. But then Ed came to faith in Christ during graduate school. All those seeds sown in church during his childhood apparently had fallen on good soil. Some seed takes more time to germinate than others. Ed's heart toward his father started softening, prompting him to go home on weekends and visit.

One Saturday night while back home, Ed jotted a note on a piece of cardboard to his father who had already gone to sleep. With little hope of it making any difference, he wrote, "Dad, if you'd like to accompany me to the 11 a.m. service at church tomorrow, wake me a little before 10:00."

To his great surprise, his father did wake him. Ed told me, "It was more out of surprise than delight that I went to church with my father that morning. I still had a long way to go in feeling any fond affection for him." This was one of those churches that offered an invitation for people to receive Christ every week. Every sermon ended with the words, "If you'd like to receive Jesus Christ as your Lord and Savior, I want you to slip out of your seat right now and come to the front of the church." Using that same phrase, Ed said to me, "*More out of surprise than delight*, I saw my father walk forward and kneel at the railing in the front of the church." After the service was over, when Ed asked him what prompted him to go forward, his father said, "Chains could not have held me back."

Perhaps Jesus' second parable about seed can help us understand Ed's father's story better. Or, more helpful still, maybe this parable will enable you to hold out hope, pray with expectation, and look for signs of growth that may have escaped your notice before now. Jesus said,

> The kingdom of God is as if a man should scatter seed on the ground. He sleeps and rises night and day, and the seed sprouts and grows; he knows not how. The earth produces by itself, first the blade, then the ear, then the full grain in the ear. But when the grain is ripe, at once he puts in the sickle, because the harvest has come. (Mark 4:26–29)

Do you note how ordinary this process seems? Commentator James Edwards observes, "A more banal comparison could not be imagined. The kingdom of God should be likened to something grand and glorious: to shimmering mountain peaks, crimson sunsets, the opulence of potentates, the lusty glory of a gladiator. But Jesus likens it to *seeds*. The paradox of the gospel—indeed, the scandal of the Incarnation—is disguised in such commonplaces."[1]

In the daily rhythms of ordinary life, sleeping and rising, night and day, the kingdom of God advances, even if we know not how. Ed wonders how much the weekly rhythm of his mother and his going to church may have spoken volumes to his grumpy father. The seed of the kingdom can break through the hardening forces of alcohol, tobacco, television, and even the affectionless disdain of a son who goes off to college and wants little to do with a father back home.

The third parable may be the most encouraging of all. Jesus told us the kingdom of God

> is like a grain of mustard seed, which, when sown on the ground, is the smallest of all the seeds on earth, yet when it is sown it grows up and becomes larger than all the garden

---

[1] James R. Edwards, *The Gospel according to Mark* (Grand Rapids, MI: Eerdmans, 2002), 142.

plants and puts out large branches, so that the birds of the air can make nests in its shade. (Mark 4:31–32)

Here, Jesus offers a more illustrative way of saying what the parable of the soils told numerically, that some seed will bear fruit, thirtyfold and sixtyfold and a hundredfold. What starts out as just a phone conversation, an e-mailed question, a mention of "I'll be praying for you," a gift of a book or DVD, or a note scribbled on a piece of cardboard, can bring about a widespread harvest beyond all dreams.

As Ed packed up to return to graduate school, he suggested that his father might want to call the pastor of the church and see what he recommended for growth in his newfound faith. Never would Ed have expected the program of discipleship the pastor laid out for this now sixty-year-old babe in Christ.

"Do you read the daily newspaper?" the pastor asked Ed's father. He replied that he did—every day.

"I want you to look up the listings of all the people who had babies or announced their marriages. Send them a note of congratulations along with one of these tracts." He handed him a stack of tracts and sent him on his way. That started the daily writing of notes to dozens of new parents and brides and grooms. It also inspired him to start writing tracts of his own.

At age sixty-six, Ed's father married a godly Christian woman, sold his house, bought an RV, and travelled all over the country with his new bride, distributing thousands (that's not an exaggeration!) of tracts he had written. For eighteen more years, he lived as a fearless evangelist, sharing his story and praying that his words would fall upon soil where "chains could not hold people back" from believing and, ultimately, bearing fruit a hundredfold.

My highest priority in writing this book was to encourage hope for Christians as they witness to their families. One final story girds me up as I pray for, extend love to, and search for words to say to those I know and love who still don't know the Savior.

For two whole years during World War II, the Nazis surrounded the city of Leningrad (now known by its former name, St. Petersburg). They pummeled it with shells, trying to crush the spirit of the people who lived there. Of great concern to the citizens was the preservation of the masterpieces in the Hermitage museum.[2] Before the siege took place, curators and volunteers packed up thousands of paintings and sculptures and shipped them east to be hidden in the rural countryside far from the urban museum. But they left the frames and pedestals where they were, in anticipation of someday reuniting them with the paintings and statues they once held.

To provide constant protection of the building, many of the staff of the museum, along with their families, moved into its basement. Together with Russian soldiers, they swept up broken glass, boarded up holes in walls, and removed snow that had come through holes in the roof, hoping to protect the beautiful parquet floors.

As a way of saying thank-you to the soldiers, the staff of the museum conducted tours of the building—even though the artwork wasn't there. Photographs depict knowledgeable curators standing before clusters of soldiers, pointing to empty picture frames and vacant pedestals. You can almost hear their voices describing beautiful works of art they had come to love and longingly miss. From memory, they would point out brushstrokes, marble contours, and the creative genius of the likes of Renoir, da Vinci, Monet, and Michelangelo.

The staff did this from the dual vantage points of happy memory and hopeful anticipation. They remembered what

---

[2] I first read about this story in Max De Pree's *Leading without Power: Finding Hope in Serving Community* (San Francisco: Jossey-Bass, 2003), 188. You can read much more about it in Sergei Varshavsky's *The Ordeal of the Hermitage* (New York: Harry N. Abrams, 1986).

once was and looked forward to what they hoped would someday be again.

We experience a similar duality as we live at this moment in salvation history. We remember what the world once was before the first man and woman's rebellion, and we anticipate what will someday be, after the return of Christ. We recall a creation before the fall, mostly through Scripture but also through an internal sense of how things ought to be. And we anticipate a consummation after the second coming, mostly through Scripture but also with a confidence assured by Jesus' resurrection.

In between these two bookends of biblical history is the world we live in, full of reminders of beauty and evidence of corruption. We see people who display goodness, love, and the image of God along with sin, rebellion, and brokenness. Some of those people live with us, grew up with us, look a lot like us, and celebrate holidays with us. When we share the gospel with them, we point them to the God who created everything and the Savior who will make all things new.

In a sense, witnessing to family members, close friends, and others who know us well fits into our waiting for the second coming. It's like the Hermitage staff waiting for the artwork to be restored . . . only more so.

PERSONAL REFLECTIONS